FINDING RUHI

NATURE AND NURTURE IN THE SEARCH FOR MY BIO-FATHER

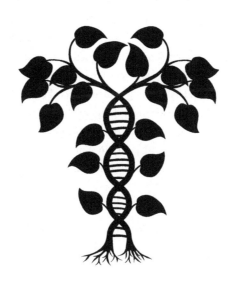

J. DYLAN MORO

Finding Ruhi: *Nature and Nurture in the Search for My Bio-Father*

Copyright 2021 J. Dylan Moro

Author's Note: Some names have been changed to protect the privacy of the people involved. I've been told by many close to me that my memory is poor, to say the least. All events of this story are true and accurate to the best of my abilities and knowledge. I have pulled from personal documentation, emails and writings of others, and conversations with those involved. My feelings and perspectives have grown and evolved on some subjects and decisions through this journey, the inevitable therapy of change. I would like to thank Susan Anderson, along with Jenny Stockdale of Cornell University, for generously granting permission to reprint in full "Pretty in Pink: Grow Edible Ginger!" (Anderson, Susan, January 9th 2012, Pretty in Pink: Grow Edible Ginger! https://smallfarms.cornell.edu/2012/01/pretty-in-pink-grow-edible-ginger/, Courtesy of Cornell University College of Agriculture and Life Sciences)

Edited by Shelley Mann.

Back cover words by Shelley Mann and Arminda Lathrop

Cover photo by Lauren Roche--Venice, Florida. Back cover photo by J. Dylan Moro—John David Moro and John Dylan Moro—Dollar Peak, Wallowa Mountains, Oregon.

FOR ZU

IF THIS BOOK FINDS YOU,
YOU CAN ALWAYS FIND ME:
(541) 908-3039.

CONTENTS

PROLOGUE

To: Dylan

Writing, for me, has to do a lot with intuition. A space open to that which is beyond words. May your words lead you to the light and the truth.

Love,
Marta

I started writing a one-page document to best be able to tell Zu about my journey someday. Words flowed from there, and writing became a sort of therapy as the story poured out.

My intention with this book is not to hurt others, not to express the one and only truth. The truth is, the truth lies in the heart and mind of a given individual.

Some truths I would like to share with you: I would not be here if things had not unfolded as they had. I believe in scientific evidence, but I can accept if others do not—it is a choice, after all. I believe my parents have always thought and known me to be theirs, and I am theirs.

My genetics are simply the code for my being, but my environment and nurture has shaped this code. Ultimately, I am the product of all of this, from a single cell to the mind that directed fingers to type this writing. Some of my qualities may be innate, some simply from inspiration and experience, but it is a cascade of spectrum. Certain percentages or numbers cannot be attached to a rating scale.

I do not yet know of a science that can say I am this way because of nature, or that way because of nurture. If I am jogging with Johnny, driving with Deb, or rolling a bike with Ruhi, I am enjoying the moment with an aim to glean the full scope of the experience and the shared time. My ultimate goal is to embrace my seconds on this earth and have a positive impact, regardless of the measurable or immeasurable amount. If I can learn from all of my parents and provide even a small piece of positive info to the next generation, be it my blood or not, maybe that is enough.

I am flawed and imperfect. Perhaps that is the very essence of being human. I am continuing to learn, and open to the possibility of new change. After all, anyone can get an unexpected knock on the door, email in the early morning, cold call on the phone, or genetic relative pop up on an online dashboard. It is up to each of us to choose what to do with that information, and whom to let into our family.

Regardless of why barriers may be in place, is it not vital to consider, perhaps, at the end of the day, we are all family and connected?

—*J. Dylan Moro*

INTRODUCTION

Mom said he looked like Jesus from the paintings in old churches. She said he was a poet. She knew him as "Ruhi," but that might have been a nickname or a pen name.

He had a first name and a last name, she believed, and both of them were like first names. He did not talk of his family. He wasn't homeless—she thought he had a home, at least—but he was a traveler.

"I'm sorry, Dylan," mom said, sharing details about the man she believed might be my biological father, details she thought she would never need to recall. "That's all I know."

Futuristic sci-fi movies of the eighties had failed to grasp the inevitable. Within three decades, common humans would have the ability to spit in a tube, drop it in the mail, and have their entire genetic code mapped out. That is exactly what I did in the fall of 2018. My life story changed forever. My family tree not only grafted a few branches but also inosculated a gemel. That's a forestry word that describes the unique situation in which the trunk pairs.

My DNA test results had come back half Jewish. Neither my father nor my mother were Jews.

In the three-and-a-half decades since my birth, I had lived within a truth that had always been presented to me as fact. I was John Dylan Moro, firstborn son to John David Moro and Debra (Brink) Moro. I have always been told that I was the reason my parents fell in love. Without me there would be no Moro family.

The story goes that on the day I was born in a modest south Portland home, rare sacred sunlight shone through the windows, making the walls of that place radiate as Johnny and Deb worked out the dynamics of his original song "Look out to Sea." The twenty-first of February, a week after my Valentine's due date, was the time of year in P-town when the sun is as rare as a chart-topping folk hit, and the nearby Pacific Ocean provides the endless rain supply pelting down on evergreen needles.

My folks gave me my dad's first and last names but called me by my middle name, Dylan, a new and unusual name for a boy in the early eighties. It was a nod to Dylan, the musician. Being musicians themselves, my parents were inspired by Bob's folk tunes and his willingness to influence a movement. When twenty-one-year-old Robert Allen Zimmerman rebranded himself in 1962, he cited the poet Dylan Thomas as an inspiration for his songwriting.

"It's a little hard to name a child together," Mom told me, much later. "I think I liked you having the same initials as Dad too."

Upon my home birth, as I was placed in the bathtub, a boisterous Johnny exclaimed, "He floats like a stick!"

Right away Pops linked my blue eyes to my paternal great-grandmother, Nana. I was theirs, they were mine, and that was all that mattered. This was the truth they chose to believe.

But now, suddenly, here was a different story. A different set of DNA. A different man, who seemed more like a mythical figure than human. Backed by genetic science, this truth felt like an alien growing inside me. Had I been naïve in not noticing how I had slightly different physical features, behaviors, interests, and personality traits from my three siblings? Honestly, these differences were unremarkable to me as well as to others, and anyway I shared many similarities with my sisters and brother. But now my known origin story was coming into question.

On the phone with Mom, I took a breath and asked, "How do I track a person down without a name or a location from nearly four decades later?"

"By now he's passed away," she replied. "A friend told me he had died."

I processed this and paused again.

"What friend told you that?"

"She's passed away as well now, Dylan, I'm sorry."

My mom gave me the woman's name, and after some Googling I found she was still alive and well, living in Portland. Months later we would sit at her kitchen table, she and my mom happily reunited, but she had no new information for me. This was another dead end, as would become the norm, on my journey of trying to find a man with no name.

By now, from what my mom could estimate, he would be in his mid to upper seventies. I had trouble imagining someone surviving that long as a vagabond wanderer. Where would he be now? It would have been easier to accept the finality of death, but my mind would not allow it.

His name was Ruhi. And perhaps, as he would later state, "It doesn't matter."

Perhaps it does.

CHAPTER ONE

ZUZU'S PETALS

By providing a saliva sample for an at-home DNA test kit, I had unknow-ingly brought to light a life-altering mystery. I craved some sort of clo-sure, even though I could recognize the idea of pursuing closure was self-serving. If I were in the situation of my theoretical biological father, I thought, I would want to know. I might even go so far as to say I would deserve to know.

I had another more important, and less self-serving, reason to pur-sue this trail. My wife, Keena, and I were expecting Zuzu, our firstborn daughter, in the year to come. I needed to be able to tell my daughter who she was—the full story—to avoid finding her in the same situation I found myself in, a generation later.

My mom had one more piece of info on this mystery man.

"He gave me a poetry book," she said. "*Petals of Light* by Ruhi. I have it tucked away somewhere, maybe that will be the way we find him."

I knew my mom, and I knew myself. I knew if I was committed to finding him, I would do all I could, and she would do all she could to sup-port me. As would my dad, Johnny, and my siblings Jerri, Julian, and Lena. Keena, I knew, would be my sounding board of reasonability and love, just as she has been since I met her a decade ago.

So off I went. I started with nightly internet searches for a face I didn't know. I was attempting to track down a wandering poet who went by "Ruhi" and was in Portland, Oregon, circa 1982. All of my information predated the very internet I was going to use as my main tool. Finding him seemed highly unlikely. What possible trace could be out there?

It didn't matter, I was driven. I wouldn't stop until I exhausted all potential avenues toward finding the truth. I was doing it for myself, for Ruhi, and for Zuzu.

LAME JOKEƨ & NAMING NAMEƨ

The moment my life changed forever, Keena and I were en route to Des Moines to meet our newest niece.

We were excited to share in the magical moment with first-time parents Brook, Keen's younger sister, and her husband, Jose. I had been fortunate enough to marry into the Byrd fam, and Evie was just as lucky to be born into the family as the first grandchild. Evie was the first niece on the Byrd side but the second niece for Keen and I. My younger sister Jerri was born eighteen months after me in November of '84, which meant we were about as far apart in age as Keena and Brook. Jerri and husband Greg were raising their daughter, our first niece-Jeanmarie in Southwestern Utah with Zion National Park in the near distance.

As we crossed the state line into Iowa, a notification popped up on my phone saying my 23andMe results were complete. Keen and I had sub-mitted separate saliva samples a few weeks earlier. As one of the leading at-home DNA testing companies, 23andMe's emphasis on genetic health conditions played perfectly into our shared nursing background. The other most popular DNA company, Ancestry.com, had cornered the family tree research part of the market.

Without thinking twice, I opened up the app. I felt excited. I couldn't wait to run the results back to Pops, breaking the news that it wasn't Native Incan or Mayan blood that ran through us but something more common like Spanish or Portuguese.

I had long imagined in myself some type of genetic lineage more similar to my brother-in-law Jose, a Venezuelan immigrant. For years I consistently bragged about sharing Jose's Spanish roots without tangible proof, comparing our skin hues and attempting broken Spanish. But I was certain our buddy bond would be strengthened even further when my results showed that through my dad's side I was, in fact, more like the "Juan" to his Jose than the John.

Throughout that year, I had been wearing out the lame joke that I was "halfway to seventy." At age thirty-five, I had unflinching confidence in who I was, nurtured by the relentless and often completely biased and unreasonable support and love of my parents. I also knew exactly what I was made of—my blood was Italian, Mexican, and German. Pops humbly bragged all throughout my life that we may have a dash of Aztec Indian as well.

I had always been curious about just how much Incan or Mexican ancestry made up my genetic code. The percentages of my cultural lineage were mysterious, but regardless of our internal differences, I shared a life-long connection with my dad. A Google search for the name John D Moro produces two digital white page contacts, my pops and myself. If one's name can help define their potential talents, I seemed destined for songwriting and poetry. At thirty-five, my natural skill with the written word was less than decent at best, and surpassed by my nurtured appreciation of the art of crafting a song and verse.

BOSTON AND JEWS IN NY

In 2015, three years before I would take the 23andMe DNA test, Keen and I traveled to Boston so she could run the world-famous marathon. She was fresh off an ACL surgery three months prior. Her surgeon and physical therapist said there was no way she was going to run it. It's too soon, they said, and she wouldn't have the strength or ability. When it comes to her limits, tell Keena no and prepare to be proven wrong.

Anyway, on the trip to the East Coast we rolled down to New York City for thirty-six hours of exploration. We found ourselves in a Kosher pizza joint a few blocks from the Ellis Island ferry. We had plans to boat out to Ellis and the Statue of Liberty, but due to a bomb threat ferries were closed and instead we were going to do a Staten Island ferry to at least get a distant view. A local gave us the tip.

I had been curious to feel what my distant great-grandparents had experienced coming through to start their new lives, and standing in the same physical space seemed like the closest action we could take to emulate the experience.

We had a similar experience—with a much different backstory—as we stood over the sunken Arizona at the Pearl Harbor Memorial. It was chilling, but seemed to be the most impactful way to remember a time before Keen and I existed, as our country entered the second world war in opposition of Japan and Nazi Germany. On our boat ride out that day, we were the only two English-speaking Americans. Sharing such a somber experience with all Japanese tourists was a unique experience, but in a certain sense seemed healing. My maternal grandmother's parents were matched in an arranged marriage between two German families. My mom told me Grandma Lena's folks met on Christmas Eve and were married on New Year's Eve. Lena's mother, Marie, traveled seventeen days across the sea, Ellis Island health check, and then took a train to Mitchell, South Dakota.

My father's maternal side had rolled north from Mexico via Tucson, Arizona, to southern California. Nana, Alti Gracia Yoldi Olivas, thought to have "gifted" me my blue eyes, would not be a historical family figure to research at Ellis, but I assumed Johnny's paternal Italian side may have come through en route to Chicago. Moro family details are a bit fuzzy in general, but with fun specific stories, like the family legend of my grand-father's family sharing an apartment complex with Al Capone.

Prior to the ferry departing, at the Kosher pizza joint a block from the docks, I stumbled into a series of uncomfortably stupid questions with the man behind the counter. I asked him to help clarify the difference between Jewish religion, ethnicity, and culture surrounding the term Kosher. These questions, like so many for me, poured out faster than I absorbed the answers on the other side. So, I cannot state with clarity his answer other than that being Jewish is passed down from one's mother. Well, not of my concern then, nor was it of concern to my Irish-Scandinavian bride Keena.

We enjoyed a slice or two and held the door for a couple of dudes with tall top hats and curly sideburns. Once on the ferry we looked at the statue and Ellis and hypothesized about what it might have felt like to approach the shores of a new life. I didn't think twice, at the time, of what the truth might have been about my bloodline's specific Ellis Island experiences.

CHAPTER TWO

DNA Rejultj and Rationale

On the way to the hospital to meet Jose and Brook's firstborn little Venezuelan beauty Evie, I clicked on the DNA breakdown. Northwestern European 51.3 percent—makes sense, a bit more Deb than Johnny, I thought. But I was perplexed by what came next: 48.7 percent Ashkenazi Jewish.

My first reaction was, okay, this thing is a farce. How accurate could a test tube of saliva really be? They're new to the game of DNA mapping; my spittle must have been cross-mixed with some Jewish dude's.

A quick Google search for "people using 23andme and getting back incorrect Jewish DNA" returned plenty of skeptics. A lady found out she was half Jewish when she knew she was not. Several conspiracy theories popped up, such as the company itself was run by Ashkenazis who were oversimplifying the genome process to prop up their genetic dominance.

I wasn't convinced, but it did prompt me to entertain a little conspiracy theory of my own. My maternal German grandmother, Lena, must have been actually Jewish, whether she knew it or not. After all, I got my thick, wavy, curly hair—my "Jew-fro" through college—directly from her.

Lena was the product of an arranged marriage between German family friends. Was it not possible that the arranged marriage was between Jewish refugees? Lena's father Carl, hard of hearing and vision, was ready for a bride. Marie was asked, along with her sisters, who would like to take the leap of faith and travel to the United States to be wed to a farmer in Letcher, South Dakota? Lena tells the story that when Marie was first introduced to Carl, she was relieved to find out he was the taller of the brothers.

So, there it was for me. A simple answer. Marie and Carl were both actually Jewish escapees from the war. Sure, Marie's uncles were soldiers in the war in Germany, but just like in movies I had seen, they must have actually denounced the Nazi movement and been looking to protect and save as many Jews as possible. And I, through my grandmother, was a modern-day beneficiary of this bravery. Or conversely, they were simply Nazi soldiers serving their country's will.

Easy fix, I thought. I would start a group text with all my cousins on my mother's side asking if anyone knew of any Jewish DNA in our family. Surely someone had done a DNA test and had found the same results as me. Or perhaps someone knew the true secret of the arranged marriage. I had a wide swath of cousins, grandkids from Lena and Gerrit's six children. Text sent. Now I just had to wait for this exciting story to be confirmed. I had uncovered an amazing truth about our family, I thought—my grandma's bloodline was actually the product of rescued Jews.

There was one piece of scientific fact yakking in the back of my skull, however. Having taken courses on basic genetics and even taught about it, I knew only around one-fourth of one's DNA is a result from each grandparent. I was pushing the halfway mark in terms of 'Jew goo.' That meant Gerrit, Lena's German/Dutch husband of nearly seventy years (with baseball mitts for hands distal to his six-foot-seven frame), must have some Jewish DNA as well.

Potentially even more interesting—what if the Aztec Indian Johnny had always talked of with a proud smirk was actually Jewish DNA? I could easily make the leap that my pops looked as Jewish as he did Middle Eastern or Hispanic. He seemed to be able to fit any phenotypical mold. With these potentials and some quick math, my deoxyribose is pushing fifty percent Jewish. Plus, that nice golden tan I could produce in the summer could be the proud mix of my pops' olive skin (whiter after years under the clouds on the rainy Oregon coast) and my northwestern Euro lineage.

It was all adding up. No worries that my sister Jerri's beautiful large eyes were spitting images of Johnny's, and that she had the token Moro olive skin. Or that Jer and Greg's daughter Jeanmarie was a phenotypical Moro. Displaying the exact same features as her mother and her maternal grandmother, she could reel one in immediately by batting her long lashes over large brown eyes.

My youngest siblings, though, were lighter-skinned "whities." At six-foot-six, my brother had a stretched-out version of my build, with frail shoulders, hunched back, long legs and gangly arms. These results seemed an easy surprise to solve.

CHAPTER THREE

CRICKETS FROM COUSINS / POSSIBLE PHENOTYPIC RATIONALE

I kept waiting for cousins to respond on the group text—crickets. No one was jumping on the Jewish bandwagon. I started to process what this might mean, what the true options for answers might be:

a. 23andme was jacked up and incorrect.

b. The results were correct. There was Jewish DNA on my maternal side and maybe even a little bit from my pops. So, I might be able to stretch myself to nearly 50 percent Jewish, as I strongly seemed to take after my mom's side of the family.

c. The results were correct. Hard to put into words, but perhaps my reality would be forever shifted.

I struggled to take option C seriously. For thirty-five years I had woken up knowing who I was and what I was made of. As long as I can remember I would look at my face in the mirror and be able to attribute physical features to my parents. It wasn't a major deal, something I did without giving much thought.

Blue eyes? My parents made it immediately clear they were connected with my dad's grandmother, Nana, in Tucson. A skinny, slowly developing frame? My uncles were slow to grow as well, my mother assured me. Many family members on both sides were lean, and my own dad had chicken legs made sinewy with years of running, biking, and hooping.

As I aged, the balding game caught me. This one was easy. I had for years given my dad the business about his bald spot, knighting him with the endearing nickname of "Baldy." Besides it's more myth that baldness runs on the mother's side. Modern science was showing more and more there is paternal balding influence.

My pear-shaped body and hunched shoulders, in some ways, represented both sides. There were tangible contradictions, though. Nobody else rocked my frail frame. Julio was a lurch of a larger Johnny with the same barrel-caged chest and gangly arms. Youngest sister Deebs was a high school state champ sprinter, with strong, fit legs and lean upper body. My male cousins were broad and strong.

Even my dad's long arms hung from wide shoulders that had benefited his wrestling career and old man hoops glory games. Johnny's post-cancer fight and years of chemo had "E.T.'d" his body, leaving his skinny arms and legs attached to a well-built chest cavity with powerful lungs. This respiratory factory of CO_2 and oxygen exchange had served his endurance sports well through the years. His shoulders were bony with some forward hunch, maybe enough to rationalize a connection with my poor kyphosis posture.

KEEN'S DNA KIT

Keena had also submitted her tube of saliva to 23andMe, and her results came back around the same time. In some ways I was hopeful at that point that Keen's would come back partially Jewish as well, after finding several postings discussing DNA inaccuracies from samples being classified as specifically Ashkenazi Jewish, unbeknownst to the saliva senders. This would be the easiest explanation for me. The science behind the seemingly all-too-easy genetic company would then seem inaccurate, tainted, and misleading.

Keena's came back exactly as we had predicted. Half Irish, with a splash of German and Scandinavian, "broadly northwestern European." Keena even had 2.6 percent Southern European—Spanish and Portuguese, as compared to my zero percent Southern European. How was this possible? I was the *Ese*, I had the Spanish Italian, Aztec Indian Mexican father. Her maternal grandmother was an O'Flanagan who married a Swedish man, and her father's side were German transplants to the Dakotas.

Again, I assured myself, my test must simply be tainted. My tube was switched in the lab and someone else was getting results showing a Mexican/Italian like myself. This happens to identical twins in the nursery—surely a couple of plastic vials of spit could easily be swapped.

CHAPTER FOUR

GENETIC TESTING BACKSTORY

I had first heard about 23andMe in the summer of 2014 while doing a science training at Sanford Labs in Sioux Falls, South Dakota. One of the instructors casually mentioned that she was thinking of having her DNA mapped out to find out where her ancestors were from.

This blew my mind. As a skeptic, I wasn't totally biting, but the potential seemed crazy. She generally described this process where a company could take your DNA and give you a result. I assumed a blood sample or some piece of flesh, but she said no. Just buccal cells scraped from your cheeks by swishing some special salted liquid.

Turns out it was even more simple. All that was required was some spittle. She mentioned a friend who had done it with almost a hint of braggadocious mystery, like it was an exclusive club or unique adventure. I still couldn't fully grasp. Even if "they" could isolate my DNA, how could "they" connect that to my country of original lineage? Was DNA marked? Had it been mapped using certain humans with DNA samples?

In short answer, yes, but it was all more complicated than that. It's a science frontier that is still being pushed towards perfect accuracy. I locked in my memory the thought of pursuing this different form of adventure, but it took four years and a special half-price offer on genetics and health history to sparked me to ask Keen, "Hey, you want to try one of these genetic tests?"

Knowing the science might not be enough to motivate her, I added, "It has some type of health history that shows if you're predisposed to certain genetic conditions. It might be a cheap, easy screener for future kids."

SCREENING THE GENES

In that very same biomed course, I had been trained to teach and was introduced to the idea of DNA tests. I would play a documentary for my students called *Mapping the Human Genome*. The video was made in the early 2000s, but it dove into the massive process and human hours spent using giant computers to solve and sequence the human genome. A generation later, these at-home DNA kits used a similar technique.

Sequencing the first human genome required multiple labs coordinating efforts over a decade, and had a price tag of a cool $1 billion. The at-home kits used genotyping, a slightly different and more efficient process, and provided results in a few weeks to month priced in the $100 range.

The part of the video that really stuck with me was an interview with twin brothers who married two women who were also close friends. This made for a tight-knit family, with best friends sharing twin spouses— sounds confusing. Based on how they described their small college and privileged lives, I imagined they all met at a small Northeastern school. The brothers had a nerdy, almost soft demeanor as they described starting out their lives as parents and uncles to each other's children.

One brother discussed the call he received from his twin expressing updates on his eldest daughter, who was progressing normally as an infant but had started to regress and was now losing verbal and visual tracking abilities. She had been diagnosed with Tay-Sachs disease. From this point, I was humbled down from the natural perch of judgment where I often live my life.

The narrator then described this disease that, to me and my advanced science high-schoolers, seemed the worst of the worst. Essentially children appear normal for X amount of time and then their brain begins to turn to mush, at first slowly then exponentially more rapidly. They lose all function and control of what they once had. They become vegetative, inevitably giving way to respiratory death. And, of course, it was incurable.

The uncle of the recently diagnosed young girl described how he had talked with his wife, and they as a family decided to move closer to his twin to help support his family through this tragic diagnosis and unavoidable process. As he shared, his voice cracked and the video panned to his wife. She stated she had been in touch with her best friend, who, in detail, described some visual cues and lack of motor response that her sick daughter had shown. It was then that the wife of the uncle twin said she had noticed similar qualities in their newborn son. This prompted the parents to do follow-up testing, which came back with the heavy news that their son had Tay-Sachs as well.

The storyteller, I remember, used the phrase, "a cruel twist of genetic fate." The first family with the older daughter had a second son who did not have Tay-Sachs; a genetically recessive trait that had a one-fourth chance of being passed down to offspring if both parents are indeed carriers.

One can get into the nitty-gritty science of Tay-Sachs disease by simply Googling, and find the highest at-risk group is Ashkenazi Jews. Both the twins and their wives were all Jewish, and all unknowing carriers of this tragic recessive gene.

It was hard to watch without putting myself in their shoes. I played the video twice a year for four years, and by about the third or fourth viewing it was easier to dismiss. I simply thought, well, no worries in my case, I'm not Jewish. I am a German/Dutch/Mexican/Italian whose alter ego is simply *Ese* because of my ironic Mexican heritage.

My brother-in-law Jose had long been my reprieve and confidant in the Byrd family. Marrying sisters can connect men in a way that is immeasurable. This bond becomes exponentially more solid when those dudes spend time hanging on long bike rides or, say, on a road trip around the western U.S.

As part of our brother-in-law bonding, Jose and I trash-talk each other about anything. Nothing is off limits. Hence to Jose I was simply *Ese*, and to me he was, of course, my counterpart Mexican gangbanger, *Ese*. Leaning in on multicultural jokes, my longstanding tasteless joke was that the Byrd girls had tried to out-diversify each other in terms of their choices in mates. Eldest Keena had chosen a semi-safe play, German/Italian with a splash of Mexicano. Brook broke the domestic barrier by linking with a bilingual Venezuelan transplant. Youngest sister "Tuna" went for the long ball grand salami with a Puerto Rican-African called Toney.

The most inappropriate and culturally insensitive part of my terrible joke was then to clown on the solo son of the Byrd family, known as "Chrissy-Poo." He kept it safe, simple, and close to home by marrying a cute and competitive little blonde-haired, blue-eyed homegrown South Dakotan, Claire. Simply just linking her hair and eye color, I put it, "Chris chose der Führer's physical dream specimen." I am now rightfully ashamed of this completely messed up "joke".

For me, it was a nonchalant form of acceptance to make an uncomfortable point of joking about the rudest, crudest, and most socially unacceptable topics. I grew up hearing Jewish jokes, and didn't think much of it. What do Jews and pizza have in common? I won't finish that tasteless joke, or tell you about the time someone messed up throwing the label: "Jewed, screwed, and tattooed." I didn't pause to think of the potential irony of these terrible jokes, or what it would be like to stand in the shoes of a Jewish person. Heck, I literally did not know any Jewish people.

In college, I grew a mop of hair over a two-year period, thick curls that gave me a few extra inches. My grandma Brink, a German descendant with a heart of gold, would tell me that we had the same hair. I agreed. My college buddies simply called it my "Jew-fro." I took that as a compliment. It was my trademark look under a backwards hipster trucker hat, a two-dollar purchase from Goodwill. I embraced the look as interesting and cheesy in an attempt to be ironic. In my mind (and undoubtedly no one else's) I pulled off the delicate balance between poverty and style, an intriguing place I wanted to live.

If I couldn't stand out because of God-given physical strength, as my pops had been able to in his early twenties, I'd just simply "put a little lipstick on the pig" to garner potential interest from co-eds. My brother-in-law Chris even went as far as to call me cheap in my mid-thirties, going on a rant about how I handled money. He went on about how I was unwilling to shell out extra Benjamins for small, common things. This lined up in complete congruence with my college reputation as well. If there was a dime to be pinched, I was going to use every ounce of my inherently puny thumb and pointer finger to pinch, nay squeeze, away.

I would joke it was the Jew in me, not really giving thought to what this phrase meant, not really considering my own unbeknownst Jewish stereotypes: curly hair, nerdy physical stature, ironic wit, and love of a good deal. I just tended to go looking for the best clearance rack jeans at the already clearanced store—even if they fit just a few sizes too big—and attributed that to the fact that I grew up financially poor. We were rich in time and love, but if my parents were arguing it was about spending habits and how ends were not going to meet that month.

MISPLACED CULTURAL D-FENCE

At times I would defend Mexicans, for instance when some dude was making racist jokes, doing impersonations, or dissing the migrant workers at the chicken farm near my middle school. I would simply fire back, hey dude, I'm Mexican. My grandma's family was from south of the border, like Pablo, the other red-nosed reindeer. Even if only momentarily, a look would cross their faces that said, "oh, my bad," as they looked at my white skin and, from my perspective, a nearly mirrored version of themselves.

I would even take it a step further with a check mark, just a micro-cosmic way to stick it to a system that tried to box people into certain categories. From my late teen years on, I always looked for the box that said White Caucasian of Hispanic Origin and, with a sly smile, placed my bold check or X.

It wasn't exactly a point of pride linked to my Mexican heritage, because if my inner self's little voice was being honest, it felt like a loophole in self-declaration. It was my tiny way of empowering a race that seemed easily dismissed by many privileged white people I grew up with. I felt like a spy behind enemy lines.

The thing was I didn't have a strong connection to Mexican culture. I enjoyed the food okay, but I hardly spoke Spanish and had never even traveled to Mexico. My grandmother was fluent, and my father claims he audibly understood but could not speak with fluency. He had a dogged understanding of commands but was unable to communicate back. So the bilingual buck stopped with me and my siblings.

In reality, I didn't feel as much like a double-agent spy as an imposter who had the ability to put on a different hat when it was beneficial for self-ish reasons. This is where the ironic "Ese" banter would come from years later with Jose. I was poor at Spanish II in high school, but I clumsily tried to speak with his non-English speaking Venezuelan parents. I tried to use my broken Spanish again while ordering some paella in Barcelona, and my language skills reached the point of destruction while ordering grilled cheese bites in Portuguese at the 2016 Olympics in Rio, Brazil.

Either way, I thought I was bloodline-entitled enough to be able to claim my Mexican or Spanish heritage when it was convenient to me—even though I had no true, viable connection to the culture save for holidays spent with my relatives in Covina, California. There, we shared some "Hispanic Mexi-Italiano" dishes, and I joined in the family production line for my fam's favorite: tamales. I was the weak link. I wasn't quite patient enough to be able to tie the corn husks proficiently, and also had no real feel for the proper disbursement of masa-to-meat-to-cilantro ratio.

No worries. Eskimos didn't live in igloos, and American Indians didn't live in teepees. I didn't have to fulfill every stereotype of my lineage.

It was hard, though, not to consider if I'd fulfilled any?

BACK TO TAY-SACHS

Since I wasn't Jewish, I wouldn't have to worry about Tay-Sachs. A quick internet search didn't turn up much in terms of genetic diseases specific to the German/Italian/Mexican realm. Jewish people had, unfortunately and seemingly unintentionally, cultivated that particular genetic tendency through close family marriages and avoiding interfaith (mixed) offspring. This purity of bloodline allowed for the recessive trait to be passed in as many as one of every twenty-seven Ashkenazi Jews.

I sang the song "If I Were a Rich Man" and watched *The Fiddler* a couple times in sixth grade, so I completely understood the Jewish culture, right? Wrong. Adam Sandler's Hanukkah song filled in the cracks of what I didn't get from Norman Jewison's 1971 Broadway adaptation, but the glaring truth was that I was as uneducated about the Jewish culture as one would expect from a boy growing up without any Jewish people in my life. Zero.

Needless to say, I didn't need to sweat these twins' tragic story.

CHAPTER FIVE

PREP FOR KIDS, KNOWLEDGE IS POWER

All the same, it wouldn't hurt Keen and I to do a little investigation into any odd recessive health risks we may or may not be carrying. In researching about Jews and Tay-Sachs, I had found an article about the disease along with other recessive diseases that show up in the Irish, which is Keena's background.

Meanwhile, I still grappled with the sentiment of how accurate the test could be. Having a background in science and nursing brought out my inner skeptic. Some random company using the U.S. Postal Service to gather saliva tubes couldn't accurately depict health concerns. It takes a doc's office, thorough family history, and blood samples going to high-tech labs to determine things of that nature, right?

The health-concern angle might, however, serve as enough kindling to motivate Keen to try the kit that had been marinating in the back of my mind for the last four years as a different form of adventure. The twenty-year-old Tay-Sachs video made mention that someday in the near future, all people would be able to map out their individual genome. That day had arrived.

ADVENTURE AND EXPERIENCE OF THE INTERNAL

Throughout my twenties, I pursued any adventure or experience possible. A volunteer trip to eastern Africa? You bet. Graduate assistant coaching in Hawaii? Yes please. Nursing internship in Anchorage? Sign me up. It is said traveling is contagious, as is the feeling of adventure one gets by being a unique entity in a different setting.

The genetic test presented a different type of adventure. It was internal. It would answer the simple question of what exactly is the "stuff" within? This experience would take place in both the mind and the body. The blueprints that shaped who one becomes were long written within nucleic base pairs—at least, this is the way science has explained it.

I had heard a *Radiolab* on a group of people in a small Scandinavian province who suffered a four-year drought and, thus, food shortage. This lack of food had produced markers on their genes that coded for the adaptation to overcome more brittle bones and lack of vital muscle protein in future-generation offspring. It was similar to tree rings showing a history of smaller years of growth due to lack of resources.

During this group of people's lives, it appeared, their DNA had accommodated for the potential of environmental issues for their genetic lineage. In other words, nurture had affected nature.

I wondered if other groups of people had similar markings in their genetic code based on environmental factors. Jewish people during the Holocaust, African people during slave trade, even something as simple as athletic people procreating with other athletes. There have been studies showing certain genes that code for dealing with stress have been activated in subsequent generations of Holocaust survivors.

23andme had cited different historical figures as being genetic reference checks for the DNA of modern-day humans. Genghis Khan's DNA could lend insight to current lineage based on specific chromosomal markers found in as many as 13 million different men. My results showed that Napoleon Bonaparte was a distant relative.

All of that was fine, but what DNA within my cell's nucleus, as it unwound, replicated, and split, made me who I am? Also, what percentage of this genetically predetermined substance affected my emotions, or influenced my decisions? Was my mind at bay to my DNA? Or will my life's experience mark my own DNA for future generations?

These were questions of control, and I could use my parents as case studies to lean in or away from certain traits. However, being able to separate natural qualities versus those of my environment remained challenging, as they were intertwined within my "nuclear family."

THE SCI-FI FUTURE OF GENETICS

The other video I would play for my students during our genetic section was *Gattaca*, a late-nineties sci-fi. The film played with the idea of a generation that could choose to genetically manipulate offspring, pulling the best genes to the top of the petri dish and essentially creating the ultimate child. Natural-born children had started to become obsolete, and they were unable to compete both in athletics and the workforce. The movie follows a set of brothers as they navigate life. The younger brother was genetically engineered and the elder was the last of a dying breed of natural-born, who overcomes a heart disorder to pursue a career in space flight.

I had seen the movie as a teen with my pops and was left with the impression of, what a cool idea. I found myself pulling for the older brother, the genetic underdog. I wonder if, at the time, my dad might have considered my genetics. I wonder, if he had been given the opportunity, would he have tried to bring out the best? I doubt it, considering my parents' naturopathic approach to life, avoiding hospitals and medication and opting for home births for me and all my siblings. Maybe just the genetic code for a supreme "sky hook," a la Kareem.

Later, as an educator and when considering starting my own family, I would pose the question to students. How would they feel if one day they were presented with the ability to manipulate their kid's DNA? The majority, of course, were against it, but things changed when I questioned the topic of genetic diseases such as Tay-Sachs, PKU, or Down syndrome. The students would get a pondering look as they reconsidered their original thoughts. Where is the line between providing a child health benefits and playing God?

Many students would settle on the thought that if genetic modification could benefit health it was okay, but anything more than that was too far. The devil's advocate retort then would be, well, is fair skin an issue when it comes to sunburns? Could height or muscle makeup help to promote a better experience in sports and perhaps lead to healthier lifestyles and self-confidence? Is mental health worth considering? If so, would one feel more gratification from job performance when given better genetic tools to reach a higher potential?

The slope was slippery.

CHOOSING A FAM

Ignorance is bliss. It seemed not having the option to manipulate the DNA of one's offspring made life less complicated. It was easy to appreciate the genetics I was born with—I was just thankful to be alive. Humans tend to rationalize their situations one way or another, applying a positive or negative spin.

The child created has no choice when it comes to genetics. I had, at times, played with the abstract thought of humans in another, pre-life universe choosing the family they ultimately wanted to belong to. Sitting at a desk, flipping through pages, much like an adoption agency. The glaring fallacy with this theory was the reality of destructive home situations that random lives are brought into each day. Why would someone choose a life of immediate suffering?

I rested easy in the comfortable situation I was born into, both in terms of genetics and environment.

CHAPTER SIX

REALITY OF KIDS HEALTH

This is all fun food for thought when it is hypothetical, but things become less clear when you're in a doc's office discussing the Down syndrome screening tool that you volunteered to sign up for as soon-to-be first-time parents, thinking it a wise decision. And the screening test is positive.

This screening test had much lower diagnostic accuracy than the amniocentesis that would eventually be done. In other words, there are many false positives in the screening that trigger a more dialed-in diagnostic test. We were fuzzy on our understanding of this at the time, and it triggered some questions. We thought we had been responsible waiting to get our life in a healthy place to provide for children—we were financially set up with a comfortable home and established careers—but had we actually been more selfish in waiting for pregnancy, thus increasing potential health risks? What life were we setting our offspring up for? The age-old question, what world were we bringing kids into?

Should we have adopted? We discussed adoption at length and were inspired by those who had made the decision to provide a stable home environment to a child in need. The movie *Lion* perhaps put it best for both of us:

"Because we both felt as if ... the world has enough people in it.
Having a child couldn't guarantee it will make anything better.

But to take a child that's suffering like you boys were. Give you a chance in the world. That's something."

Regardless, it was a kitchen talk at my Grandma Lena's home in Plankinton with my close cousin SaLena that gave me the ultimate perspective. SaLena has raised twin boys, one with Down syndrome. Her son and other children with the disorder, she said, make every other life they come in contact with richer thanks to their humor, kindness, and appreciation.

I had a close friend group in high school and one of our buddies at school was Anthony, who was a few years older, and had Down's. He made each of our days that much more enjoyable. So, as we awaited the results from the diagnostic test of our firstborn, who would be Zuzu Byrd Moro, who had beautiful 3D ultrasound lips and a little nose, we had the perspective to know it would be great no matter the diagnosis. She would enrich our lives inherently and we would give our best to do the same for her. In the end the amniocentesis was negative for Down syndrome.

ME IN UTERO / JOHNNY'S DREAMS

My mother's first pregnancy was a bit different than Keen's in terms of phase of life, but similar in commitment to providing the most loving future to her firstborn. When Mom found out she was pregnant, she spent the summer with her parents near Steamboat Lake in the Colorado Rockies. What brought her back to the Pacific Northwest was a phone call with Johnny. He simply asked her to move into his place in Portland, Oregon, for the remainder of the pregnancy and go from there.

My mom has told me my entire life that I was the reason they fell in love, and without me there would be no other siblings. She has been the ultimate in terms of providing me with, at times, irrational self-confidence through positive support and complimentary love. So much so that I sometimes dismissed her kind words. Well, she is my mom, that's what they do. I know I'm not the greatest songwriter, nor do I have one of the nicest smiles, nor am I the primary reason my parents fell in love. She is simply being good to me because she has innate, unconditional love for me.

Regardless, I was aware from pictures that I was at their wedding in the fall of 1983, in a quaint little church in the forest at the base of Mt. Hood. We drove by together later in life to check it out. I also knew there was a story of her father, my Grandpa Gerrit, telling John after I was born, "You won't find a better wife than my girl Debbie."

My dad once aspired to play music and write original tunes as a profession. In fact, his move to Portland had been in large part to fine-tune some licks with his best buddy, Alan. His goal in the early eighties was to be able to gig around in the musically appreciative and perpetually rainy "Rip City."

He also did a year in Europe with buddies from southern California, and traveled back through Canada with a serious girlfriend at the time. His buddies would get together every few years to share memories and commemorate their time together in the seventies over slide shows, brews, games, food, laughter, and stories. I was the first of the next generation of Johnny's buddy group, who was as close as his family unit, hanging at the "reunion." My mom would go as far as to say that I was the reason Johnny's friends chose to have kids. Again, she is my mom, she is supposed to say things like this. The next buddy to have a son would name his first-born John.

I just remember having an awesome time hanging. I collected and dissected owl pellets from the old-growth trees at the end of the orchard property, I played Frisbee golf and horseshoes, and I watched "semi-grown" men light their farts on fire, the flames only ignited because of belly-rolling laughter. I retain the warm, peaceful feeling of lying under the stars, sleepy eyes closing to the sound of live music late into the night. The music was led by Johnny and Deb, a couple whose love language was and continues to be music.

THE NURTURE MY PARENTALS WERE GIVEN

For my parents, as it does for many, the pendulum swung far from their upbringing. Johnny's father supported his family as a barber, and his uncle was a successful entrepreneur building a beauty college, even cutting hair for the stars of southern California. At a young age my dad knew he wasn't going to live his life in the traffic and stress that comes with the city and surrounding area of Los Angeles, even if it meant moving away from his loving parents and family-first culture.

Deb grew up the youngest of six siblings, and had great support from a selflessly loving mother and tough and loving father. She found familial independence through spiritual pursuits ranging from intense Christian institutions to, later in life, the Guru Maharaj Ji's pursuit of enlightened knowledge.

In their formative years, Johnny's vital experiences may have been music and travel and Deb's connection and love. They found each other in Portland, the city of roses, in the early eighties, one getting away from the larger SoCal city life and one moving west to an up-and-coming city with a world of diversity and possibility. It was here that Deb's co-worker at the tree nursery and Johnny's best buddy, Alan, offered Deb an open room at his place to rent. Johnny wasn't far behind, also moving into Alan's place to pursue his music.

This time spent in the water tower district of south P-town was simple. Music, food, friends, and enough work to sustain their lifestyle. It was then that my parents became close. Deb knew she loved Johnny nearly from the day she met him. Johnny was more introverted when it came to communicating feelings, but had a way of expressing his love through kindness, inclusion, and music, all of which he happily shared with my mom.

My mom hadn't had a close partner in multiple years in the early eighties. She and Johnny were intimate one evening and, months later,

Debra was made aware of her pregnancy. Her firstborn, that would be me, had a Valentine's due date. Debra named me John Dylan Brink, but soon a secondary birth certificate was issued and my name updated to John Dylan Moro, a twofold tribute to Johnny and my folks' shared musical inspiration, Bob.

The double birth certificate with last name change was only brought to my attention later in life, as I pushed thirty-eight years old. I knew that Deb's father, Gerrit, had accompanied her to get the official paperwork and advised her to call Johnny and see what he thought should be on the birth certificate. Johnny had responded, "Moro."

This was a point of discussion at all, in my understanding, only because they had not yet made the commitment of marriage. They called me "Dylan" simply to avoid the inevitable nickname of "little John" that may have come from being the smaller of the Johns. This has become an ongoing joke within the family, as my brother is Julian John Moro. My best man, Will, and Keen often say everything in the Moro family gets "Johned."

This all culminated when my pops was picking on his banjo, which I'd dubbed his Great Smoky backwoods banjo, alter ego J. Davey (a play on his middle name David). As their new pup howled along with the banjo, his new name was instantly dubbed—J. Davey or, simply, Davey. So even their dog has been "Johned."

Giving a person a family name serves many purposes. It can be tribute, legacy, endearing reminder, used for sorting lineage, or a happy coincidence. I always felt my name was a purposeful honor and point of pride to fundamentally show connection between myself and my pops.

Oftentimes there is more to a name than what is written on a paper, introduced with a handshake, or found on a headstone. There is a story, a purpose, a greater bond placed upon titling a living being and spirit with a phrase to be called and referred to. My name was no different. It represented an untold or unknown story based upon acts of kindness, faith in a truth, and love.

MY ORIGIN STORY

I spent my early childhood in a comfy and peaceful two-bedroom, one bath on Southwest Pendleton Street in the water tower district of Portland.

A couple blocks to the east was the Willamette River, where twenty years later and a hundred miles downstream in Corvallis I would spend countless hours training in crew shells. We were perpetually drenched in rain, fog, boat spray, and mist for months on end in complete, socked-in cloud cover. We prayed for the rarest of days when the sun would pop out and we could take our shirts off to soak up the golden energy. We would have an annual fall regatta on the Portland loop between Lake Oswego and Oaks Park, which sits on the opposite shore from my infanthood home. As I aged, my life would continue to cycle through familiar locations and experiences.

My mom kept three daycare kids part-time in the home. She said she would take walks with the kids and our lab, Rosie, who had a big backyard to hang in, while, "Dad rocked the house with his electric guitar." Along with two bandmates, my parents formed 2 Sticks Down and would play a couple hours a few nights a week.

One of my dad's best Euro-tripping, Cali-born buddies, "Uncle" Kelly, visited from Missoula soon after I was born. After spending enough time with Johnny and Deb to see they would retire to different bedrooms, Kelly could not hold his extroverted jubilation in. Shocked, he asked my dad, "Wait, you're not sleeping with her?"

This humorous exclamation was enough to nudge Johnny to permanently make his move, and they've shared a bedroom ever since. Months later, sharing morning coffee, Johnny simply asked, "So do you want to just get married?"

This was the "music" Deb had been longing to hear, as her dream for years had been to share a family and life with Johnny. He decided to take a golden family ring and have it made into two matching rings, with simple, small diamonds placed on both. My pops shared with me the ring's history:

My Uncle Alfredo Yoldi is my grandmother Altagracia's brother. They moved to east Los Angeles, where he was a jeweler and opened up a business in downtown L.A. His wife Josephina, my grandma, and my uncle lived together after the execution of my great grandfather and my Aunt Josephina's parents during the revolution in Mexico. They lived in Tucson in between Mexico and L.A. I have always called them Nino and Nina. My Uncle

35

Alfredo made a platinum gold ring with a star sapphire and two diamonds. My aunt gave it to me when my uncle passed. It was the first time someone I was close to died, I was fourteen. It fell off my hand and the sapphire broke, so in return for the platinum a jeweler made the two rings with the diamonds.

Years later Johnny's ring would have two more defining experiences. The first was during my high school days, while he was working at the bronze foundry. He reached back behind a malfunctioning machine in the slurry room. The power kicked on and his hand was pulled into a belt, the end of his ring finger was cut off at the upper knuckle. All neighboring phalanges were broken as well on his vital, guitar chord-creating left hand. Years of painful retraining were required to give Johnny back his original and coveted guitar skills.

When the doc had to remove the gold ring in surgery, Deb tried to find some humor, saying, "What does this say about our marriage?"

Johnny's classic line in response: "It is without end."

It was my little bro Julio who, years later, would make the fateful dive in Wallowa Lake's crystal-clear waters to find the missing ring. It had slid off and sunk down months earlier during one of Johnny's early-season dips. There it was, waiting for a Moro to reunite it with the finger that it had been placed upon—sealing marriage on December 15, 1983, with infant Dylan in attendance.

CHAPTER SEVEN

FAM PHYJICAL FEATUREJ

Fast forward thirty-seven years and we are sharing family photos from that day in our family group text. Debra is beautiful and thin, with striking eyes and a giant smile. Johnny looks humble in his brown suit with tie, dark features, and a five-o'clock shadow on tanned skin.

They are holding me between them, with my big smile matching Deb's, in an all-white onesie and shoes to boot. It's hard telling where the white threads end and my pasty white skin begins. Looking closely, I can even make out my bright blue eyes in between the dark browns of both parents.

We look happy. It's a cliché, but it seems like a tipping point in the journey of sharing lives with one another. It was in my baby blues that Johnny saw instant connection, as he cited his grandmother, Nana, from Tucson as having eyes in the same bright blue hue. Being told this story throughout my life, I didn't think much of it, just that they saw physical similarities between the genetic lineage of the Moros down to me.

In the group text Deb also sent pictures from the very first meeting of the 'new' Moros (my mom and I) and Johnny's family during the holidays, and my family phenotype connection becomes murkier or, in new reality, clearer. While looking at the images of dark, tanned family members gathering for the classic couch and dinner table shots, I can almost smell the spicy and warm aroma from the Italian-Mexican dishes permeating from the kitchen.

These photo ops would continue to be recreated over the next three decades during special family events. Nana was also said to have had fair skin, something no one else in these pictures had save for Deb and myself. In these rooms filled with beautiful brown eyes in 100 percent abundance, an onlooker would not have far to stretch to simply pose the old *Sesame Street* adage:

> One of these things is not like the others,
> One of these things just doesn't belong,
> Can you tell which thing is not like the others
> By the time I finish my song?

My dad would also mention through the years that there were pale white Mexicans. He would say that the Mexican stereotypes we had accepted were not always true, as Spaniard immigrants from generations ago had long created fair-skin Mexicans.

PHYSICAL FAM FLAWS

So conceited was I in the summer of 2003 that, upon being cross-dressed in Camp Vega's Bunkle (Bunk-uncle) Beauty Contest in upstate Maine, I proclaimed, "if being attracted to my stems in heels is wrong, then I don't want to be right."

Little did I know, at the time, that there was a fundamental reason why a bunkhouse full of third-grade Jewish girls made such a warm expression on my heartstrings as they generously flooded my unexpectedly full lips (unexpected, at least, in comparison with the much thinner lips of my parentals) with the brightest of red lipstick.

Later in life, I might have been more equipped to explain why I felt a natural cultural ease with the self-proclaimed "JAPS," the Jewish American princesses whose parents were dropping a cool $10K for an eight-week camp away from the city to take pontoons cross lake for hoops and golf. I had no familiarity with this level of extravagance, but I appreciated the opportunity to be a coach and counselor during an impressionable summer. The calves, though extremely slight like the rest of my physical shell, had always reminded me of my old man's. They had the same shape, the same tan, and the same ability to endure long runs and bike rides.

There remained stark differences. My lips are fairly full, as evidenced in the Bunkle Beauty Contest cross-dressing incident. In fact, with their ample surface area my lips get so dried out I've become a Chapstick fiend. My bro Julio had similarly big lips, and we for sure shared a hunched posture.

There were similarities, though. One could argue that Julio was a stretched-out version of me, and Lena was as pasty as I was, if not more so. Jer and I just seemed like physical polar opposites. Her eye shape and color were nothing like my smaller blues. Everyone in the family had deep browns, definitely in line with the Moros' supposed Italian/Mexican lineage. Deb always told me I had the Groeber nose from Gram Lena's side of the family.

My mom was pushing six-foot and lean. It was fairly easy to see the resemblance between us in both height and smile. Especially as they pushed past their fifties, it seemed like my mom stood above my dad by an inch or so, but he always claimed six-foot as well. Either way, somewhere in early college I passed both of them up in height, which made me assimilate more to being a Brink (my maternal grandfather's side). I had my mom's father's height, even though I remained the runt of the cousin gang.

CONVERſE FAM ReſeMBLANCe
AND SPARK TO RUN

On Johnny's side, his older bro Jimmy and his twins were both pushing over six-foot as well. So there was height on both sides, hence no surprise when my little brother Julian John jumped up to a gangly six-foot-six overnight. I knew I was smaller, but at the time found subjective similarity with Johnny's slender, chicken-legged calves and, after he conquered non-Hodgkin's lymphoma, his skinnier shoulders and upper arms that looked more similar to mine than ever.

I could also see my hands and feet in my mother Debra's. We even had similar footbed imprints in our Birki's, both in size and structural shape. My mom and grandmother both told me that I reminded them of my Uncle Gary. He was a timelessly good-looking specimen that I did not fully see in the mirror, but I appreciated the sentiment nonetheless.

To go along with my delayed growth spurt was an underwhelming amount of athleticism. My dad would talk of his dunking days and five-foot mile marks. I was a lower-middle pack cross-country runner with credit card hops. One of the greatest gifts my dad gave me was teaching me to be a runner at a young age. I showed great promise as a five-year-old competing in 5Ks and pushing 10Ks in the coming years. My memories are mostly from pictures and my mom telling stories. Every time I would make the final corner in the Prefontaine Classic on the Oregon coast, she would say, older ladies would exclaim with astonishment and maybe a tinge of pity, "Oh look, here comes a little guy."

I didn't hear them, of course. At that point, I hadn't a second thought about who I was and what my place in this world was about. I was just running with my dad to prove I could finish.

CHAPTER EIGHT

SHOULD I REALLY WANT TO KNOW? MY INTRINSIC MOTOR SAYS, "YES"

Holding newborn Evie, looking down at her dark brown, half-Venezuelan eyes, made me consider more heartedly what half of the blood coursing through my veins represented.

Would a cousin come forward and say, "It's crazy, Dylan, my DNA test came back half-Jewish as well"? Or perhaps at least a quarter Jewish, and I could make up the difference from Johnny's mysterious side, where there had to be some Jewish genetics. In fact, when I first contacted my immediate family, Johnny's take was simply, "Well, I guess I must be Jewish."

My closest sibling Jer, only eighteen months younger, was not so open and hypothetical. She had a hint of sadness, questioning, angst in her voice, when she asked, "What do you think? What does this mean? Do you even really want to know?"

Fair questions, but this train of thought—pursuit of factual scientific knowledge—was at the crux. Many friends lent opinions, and many have ideas of what they would do in such a given situation. But in line with the old adage, unless you are standing in the exact shoes of the one who has to make a given decision, it's hard to say,

For me, whether by nature or nurture, it was intrinsic to push, push, push towards accomplishment, be it physical, mental, emotional, or spiritual. For many of my closest friends and family, this characteristic was a loving flaw. They both appreciated my ability to go, go, go, and also found it exhausting, exhausting, exhausting.

If I wanted to be in multiple places pursuing multiple experiences at once, fine. But it was unfair and unflattering to expect—at times demand—it of others, even forcing a sense of guilt upon those who didn't get on board with my grand scheme of plans.

JOHNNY'S GROWING UP

Johnny, as his family lovingly called him, had initially found a passion for running at all hours of the night to escape the typical madness that is the day-to-day of Los Angeles. He'd jog out on Citrus Street in the early 1970s in what was a smaller community, Covina, surrounded by orange groves. Johnny and his buddies would snag fresh fruit off the trees and bask in the year-round perfect temps.

He still says life was good in southern California when he was growing up, it hadn't yet been ruined by greed, people, and pollution. Johnny was the second of four siblings. His older hero of a bro, Jimmy, left home early to step up to the responsibility of a teen pregnancy. He had twins, John and Chris. Johnny watched Jimmy take on early fatherhood, leaving behind his dreams of playing guitar, traveling, and exploring. Observing his brother instead start a career to become productive and responsible made a strong impression on Johnny, helping guide him to a life that was about experience, nature, enjoyment, and, most notably, not being controlled by a trade or cash. Johnny was not in a rush to start a family. It wouldn't be until he was in his thirties when his life changed from traveling musician bachelor to a family man.

In his day Johnny was a California state-champ wrestler, even moving up weight classes and still producing W's. He earned a reputation as a dude that could handle his business after he broke a teammate's arm in practice.

THE RUNT

I could barely break off the wishbone in high school. In high school, in fact, I struggled to empty rainwater from paddleboats on the docks of the

Wallowa Lake Marina. My five-foot-three boss-lady Gina had no problem mustering the strength and then rightfully trash-talking me about it. Her sons, who actually filled out our work tank tops, looked on as my noodle arms hardly turned the heads of tourist girls. From then on, I opted for the full-sleeved blue insignia shirt paired with extra baggy shorts to hide my chicken legs.

I guess my mantra at the time was, "Keep 'em guessing, what they can't see, they can draw their own conclusions on." The conclusion was simple, I was literally the smallest teenager I have yet to ever encounter in my life. The only things that kept me in the game through high school were my wit and my annoying relentlessness.

As a junior in high school I was struggling to find a role on the hoops team at five-foot-four and sixty-five pounds. I had given up football years before as an undersized weakling who was using a roll of tape per practice just to keep pads in place. For these reasons and with a push from me, my mom took me to appointments at the prestigious Oregon Health and Science University (where ten years later my pops would be treated for non-Hodgkin's lymphoma). There, the doctors did some work ups to determine if I might ever try my luck at puberty or simply sit that hand of life out. The latter looked like the strong bet at this point.

Results came back that stated I was simply running behind a few years. For me, having been shorter than my younger sister Jer for as long as I could remember, it seemed longer than a few years. No worries—again, I took after my mother's side. Her brothers were late developers, as well, who as adults eventually topped out at six-foot-five. My mother's side had height spread around thanks to grandpa Gerrit's six-foot-seven genes (he was the tallest of nine brothers by a solid margin). All seven of my male first cousins towered at least three inches above me, with muscular builds, and I even had two female first cousins and an aunt who were at least equal to my six-foot, half-inch adult stature.

I looked ahead to the future knowing someday I would grow, probably...

I just attributed my lack of physical development to genetic anomaly. I had the code within my cells, it just took time and the right nutrition to unlock it. Great things come to those who wait. I was partially correct.

PRE-DESTINY VS. REALITY

At the time, in my mind, I was the next Pre (Steve Prefontaine). The fact that I was from his hometown made all the difference—I was running the same streets he had trained on.

That salty coast town nurtured me into running, and this was ever more valuable than my natural abilities. The running culture and nurture were there, plus I had my dad's nature, so I was destined for greatness. Fast-forward ten years and I was a middle pack, small-town cross-country runner, captain of the team coached by my pops.

Fast-forward another decade or so and I was attempting to pace Keen in marathons to meet her Boston qualifying time standard. Pacing poorly. The day before the Honolulu Marathon, I signed up because my nursing shift was canceled on New Year's due to low census. Keen had been modestly training in between sixty-hour nursing weeks for the Army Reserve and working on her doctorate distant coursework.

I had jogged once a week or so with her, when I wasn't island hopping on quick flights to fully take in the chain (visiting every island except Moloka'i, the former leper island). And when I wasn't island hopping I was attempting to become a typical "haole" surfer, a tradition that had popped up in my life previously, with aspirations of being able to command a board and not hurt someone or myself. I had mixed results.

One go-round was highlighted with stepping on what I thought was the reef only to literally feel the sea urchin quills sticking in my foot. Some local teen surfers told me I needed to pee on the urchin spines. My immediate reaction was to say something that could get one arrested in many states, "Hey, will you guys pee on my foot, please?"

The teens gave me a WTF look and paddled away. I attempted to put my underdeveloped upper body skills to test heading to shore before I became certain I would pass out due to a reaction and drown in the shallow waters of Waikiki.

When I safely reached the shore, Keen was finishing up one of her training jogs and showed little sympathy to me as I attempted to one-leg it back to the apartment. Once researched, I used the proper treatment of vinegar, not urine (the latter was for jellyfish stings). Thankfully, for what might have turned into a pedophiliac rap sheet, the teen surfers had not obliged my request.

Keen was much more sympathetic when she jogged the three miles back to the apartment to grab our VW island wagon to pick me up at the finish line of the marathon, which had started in the dark at 6 a.m. It was now noon and she had finished two-and-a-half hours earlier. Tacking on a few extra miles to push the complete day to thirty miles wasn't a major ask in her mind (thank goodness).

I had attempted and succeeded in pacing her out for the Boston qual, at least for the first half. At the halfway turnaround I was shot. I attempted one last desperate plea to run her down so I could wish her good luck and tell her I loved her, and then the bastard of reality set in. The heat and humidity were catching up and my lunacy and general lack of respect for attempting a marathon on no training had laid out the last supper. I was to be the main course for this bastard's reckoning, and he had been fasting for days. The fact was, I deserved every ounce of the suffering. The cramping hurt, yes, each step like a knifing, but the humbling hurt more.

This marathon attracted many Japanese tourists who, I soon found out, enjoyed costuming up as much as completing marathons. I was passed by a seven-foot Darth Vader runner, a horse head I assumed was a dude underneath, a group of tutu'd ballerinas, and then the most demeaning of all. A man with a toga and wooden shoes. I could hear him coming behind me and thought for a quick sec, "Maybe there are some police men or women on horses helping with the course traffic?"

A policeman at mile eighteen, seeing my pain and sheer pathetic-ness, had asked me if I wanted a ride to the finish line. My stupidity and pride were stronger than logic and I mustered, "No, thanks."

So when I heard the hooves coming behind me, I lacked the energy to even turn backwards. Honestly, I didn't even care to know. Until he started passing me. The dude had wooden clogs. He was dressed as a historic Samurai soldier. He was running 26.2 miles in a toga on four-inch lifted blocks of wood with some twine strapped on top, and he was passing me.

Keen checked multiple medical tents for the two-plus hours I was delayed. When I finally finished, my only satisfaction was floating in the Pacific while I waited for her to come back with the car. So, to say I was destined to be Pre...was as likely as I was destined to be Jordan.

In the end I had the height-weight ratio to be a big hill ski jumper, a la a crazy person. Two damaging caveats; I was scared of heights, at least while 'flying' outside a plane, and I was lukewarm at best on a snowboard and terrible when the board was cut into two skis.

Side note, I also got third in a wife carry contest in the snow of Lookout Pass, where Montana high fives Idaho. There were three teams, and on the way back, Keens carried me. Genetic anomaly. Only so much nurture can do.

Or, as Keena's uncle Brad would later put it (in a different context), "Well, Dyl, hate to tell you but you can't make chicken salad outa chicken shit."

CHAPTER NINE

A SECOND OPINION, THE EXTREME OF OPEN TRANSPARENCY, AND INEVITABLE SCREW-UPS

No Jewish connection ever came from the cousins group text.

At the time, I didn't have any immediate relatives—that I personally knew—populate on 23andMe. Therefore I still felt like it could be a farce, a mistake, or simply inaccurate.

Fortunately, there was another well-known company out there with more of a family genealogy approach, spurred on by the Mormon church: Ancestry.com. They had a home DNA kit similar to 23andMe, with a simple saliva tube that customers mailed in.

I didn't have any hesitation in sending in my genetic code. I didn't see my genes as having some greater importance that could possibly be placed in the wrong hands, as some conspiracy theories might have one believe. In fact, several people I talked with about doing the tests said they didn't want the "government" to get ahold of their genetic code. I just joked back, "Oh ya, what are you hiding?"

THE "RIGHT STUFF"

That's all fine, but what's inside? What is the "stuff" that can't be seen? Do I have certain personality traits because of who I am genetically? Or am I the way I am because of free will, random chance, or nurture? Or is it of course a mix of all the above? For me, I've gone through life thinking of myself as a decent person, but in all honesty, I feel like my inherent good deeds seem to slip with each phase of life, every five years or so.

I knew as a young kid I was good-natured. The story goes that in kindergarten each student was asked to make a hand turkey and say what they were thankful for. I have no specific memory of this, but supposedly I said, "I'm thankful to be alive." Simple enough, but profound in terms of a humble appreciation for breath, thought, and physical shell, a gratitude for being able to interact with the world around me.

I naturally cared for others at that point in life. In my tween years, as siblings came along, I became a teaser. I was quick to try and get a rise out of others, especially my siblings. This could be seen as a defense mechanism, due to my physical shortcomings, and it's also something that many young people go through. But I have tangible memories of knowing that the balance in mental and emotional power of right versus wrong was shifting within.

Through high school I pursued academic excellence, worked to be involved in extracurriculars, and in general was kind to others in many ways—all for the self-serving gratification of being liked, awarded, and appreciated. Which, again, I recognize is natural, but I had the self-awareness to realize I was driven more by selfishness than selflessness.

Through the college years, I worked in school, but for sure leaned more toward play. On the balance, experiences, relationships, and activities carried more and more weight. I could rationalize a lower grade on a test with, "Well, I have great friends, and being part of a D-1 collegiate program is more important than sitting in the library solo endless hours."

This was a mental song and dance, as I had received the prestigious Ford Scholarship for Oregon students to stay in state and go to any college or university on a full ride. If one was able to maintain a GPA above 3.5, there were more years of grad school money to be tapped into. I knew studying general science would be a challenge, with biochem, o-chem, and physics. After my sophomore year, as I hovered around a 3.0, there was a fork in the path. I could commit myself to exhausting my energy in academia, or I could accept my abilities and enjoy the process.

The shift from pursuing "good," motivated perfection was again sliding down the backside of the mountain. I enjoyed college, while working moderately hard through courses. I wondered if my kindergarten self would have had higher standards, and questioned what was changing in me. Perhaps I was simply realizing my ceiling. Or was there something within my genes that was pigeonholing me, like the trash compactor squeezing in *Star Wars*? Was I on my inevitable path?

My parents did not complete college degrees. Pops was close, but didn't quite see through his music degree at Azusa Pacific. Instead he pursued his family's trade of hairstyling. Mom had tried a year at Northern State in South Dakota, but had a mixed experience. She was pursuing art with professors who used tough love and judgment, which did not cultivate her already questionable confidence in her abilities.

So I was the first in my immediate family to commit to finishing a degree, and only the second in my extended family. Six years before me, a cousin had graduated from the same Oregon State University, and it was sitting at her ceremony where I mentally committed. I weighed the natural pathway that people take in life with the inevitable questions one has to answer. What, in its most fundamental sense, is it important to make one's life about? Should it be about money, success, acceptance? Experience, travel, time, nature, looks, fun, faith, pursuit of knowledge, spiritual enlightenment? Family, friends, etc.?

In my youthful innocence, perhaps, I valued the things that most people would deem good. As I changed, so did my priorities. What was the cause? Was I becoming susceptible to life's vices? Was I in control, or was I predisposed to having things pan out the way they would? Did the lawyer's son produce a lawyer? Did the barber's son produce a barber?

Again, what fosters life's pursuits? Is it intrinsic within one's genetic code, or is it nurtured to the surface?

As I felt myself slipping from what seemed a good-natured human to becoming more selfish, I wondered if there was anything in my genetic code that was driving this. I also wondered if the worst thoughts that ran through my mind, the ones I imagine most people have from time to time, the ones I dismiss to focus on a positive reality, were there because I was born with them or if they were part of my nurturing. I assumed these were the things most humans struggled with while finding their life's purposes, that we're all reconciling the actions and choices we make in the moment with the ripple effect of life's path.

More importantly, though, did I have autonomous choice in these decisions, or were they in fact predetermined? Furthermore, was it God's plan at work, my environment of experiences, or simply my genes? Questions, but not always solid answers.

Dylan Thomas said, "Our discreditable secret is that we don't know anything at all, and our horrid inner secret is that we don't care that we don't."

Gabor Mate said, "In the real world, there is no nature vs. nurture argument, only an infinitely complex and moment-by-moment interaction between genetic and environmental effects."

CHAPTER TEN

THE FAM 'HONESTY' POLICY

My timeline gets a little fuzzy after we met and held Evie.

After I got my results showing nearly fifty percent Ashkenazi Jewish, I started talking with my sister Jer, working to convince her (and moreso myself) that nothing would change and the results were skewed. But one fact is always consistent within my family: honesty is acceptable as the best policy. Though we may argue, we will always remain supportive and keep our shared love intact.

Therefore, shortly after the initial cousin group text, I asked my family if any of them wanted to try the DNA test to solidify the Jewish results as accurate. In my mind, if they too showed Jewish genetics, it would verify that either: a) the company was leaning way too hard into Jewish gene-alogy and the conspiracy smoke had fire, b) we did in fact have Jewish lineage, and perhaps my grandmother's parents were Jewish refugees and/or Johnny's Middle-Eastern look was justified in Jewish genetics, or c) of which I was still unwilling to give full breath to another option.

Jer, my lifelong crutch through all the years, stepped up and said she would do it.

We shared a vast history together. In early toddler youth we dressed as clowns together, singing and passing out balloons in front of the local food co-op with our mom, aka "Ribbons the Clown." We traveled together during middle school summer, living away from our parents and siblings for three months in southern and northern California with the Moro grandparents and my pop's brother Jimmy's fam.

During high school and college years, our friends became friends. We helped each other navigate and support relationships, and pursue new experiences and fun (more support on my side in college and more judgment from me in high school). Post-college, she moved to SoDak a few months after my bro Julio and I had headed East. In my mom's hometown of "Plank," Jer got her start in education, working as an aide and eventually getting her master's as an elementary teacher. This, in turn, opened her pathway to a teaching opportunity and a move to St. George, Utah, where she would eventually raise her family after marrying a man native to the Southern "Dixie" area.

In my non-glory college days, fro'd-out and breaking one hundred pounds, when I visited my sister Jer at University of Oregon, people unfamiliar with our siblingry would think we were a couple. Weird, but I could dismiss it. It seemed to be a random guess based on how we looked nothing alike.

All good, I thought. She's the Moro—she loved tamales and salsa, and she had the ability to find the perfect joke to elicit Papa Johnny's high-pitched giggle. It was no surprise she found her spouse Greg in the hot desert of Southwest Utah.

I didn't mind the blizzards of the plains. I found my wifey back in SoDak, a few miles from where Grandma Lena and my mom had been raised in consecutive generations. If Jer was all Moro, I was leaning into all Groeber, which was Grandma Lena's maiden surname. I was slight in frame and a "late bloomer."

THE FLIP

Right around the time Jer said she was in to help with a test, I got a text from my youngest sister Lena that just said, "You should talk to mom about this, D."

So, I did. My mom showed the honesty and transparency that I had known throughout my life, providing the information that would, in turn, flip upside down the very honest and transparent narrative of who I was and had known throughout my life.

She started by revisiting a story from around the time of my early college years, a story Lena seemed to remember but that I did not recall, whether subconsciously or not.

I was in college, as the story goes, and either I do not recollect this incident or was not fully present. We were hanging in my parents' garage, converted to a family room. My youngest sister Lena, Leber-deebs as I've nicknamed her, was sitting around our family table probably plucking a guitar.

Mom had been attempting to explain why it was that she and Dad were not married when they were pregnant with me, and she had mentioned a traveling man in Portland circa 1982. Lena had asked for some clarification. Johnny had spoken up, "Debra, that's enough." He shut the convo down, and none of us worried much about it.

Mom had stayed with her parents up at Steamboat Lake in the Rockies of Colorado during the spring and summer of 1982. When she spoke with Johnny and he invited her to move back to Portland to live with him during the remainder of her pregnancy, her greatest hope was realized.

From there, once I was born and Johnny held me in the bathtub, we imprinted on one another. I was his and he was mine. That is the way Deb went on to explain it to me, later in the fall of 2018, after I'd gotten back my initial DNA results.

"Dylan, when you were born we knew you were ours. Your eyes were blue like Grandma Nana's. You were the reason we fell in love and decided to make a family. Without you, there would not be Jerri, Julian and Lena."

It started to add up, but also sent a feeling up my spine that was foreign. It wasn't anger, or misunderstanding, but somewhere in the realm of a physical feeling. I felt like I was having an internal epitome, of something making sense and seeming clear. Could it be? Was there a different explanation for my small physique, my pale skin, my lack of a palate for Mexican food, my annoying quality of always having to go go go? Was there some truth here supporting my actual origin story?

No, I mentally bristled. The tests are flawed. I know who I am. This is something one reads about or watches a flick about—not my life.

Then again, the tiny internal voice, that there was something "more" to my life—I had often dismissed the voice as an egotistical approach to life that most people dealt with—spoke with renewed momentum.

IF MORO WALLſ COULD TALK

Everyone in my entire immediate family is seemingly a musical savant, each with a special skill. Both parents can harmonize instantly, along with my sister Jerri. My dad has not picked up an instrument that he doesn't master in some sense. My youngest sister moved from the bass guitar to acoustic songwriting, even fundraising her Austrian high school exchange by selling original tunes on one of her albums. They all can strum the guitar, and with his deep range my little bro Julio does a mean Johnny Cash.

I, however, struggle with carrying a tune. It was so obvious to others that it became a great success when I was able to mask my poor singing by emphasizing a distorted, raspy vocal tone to create originals within my lack of range. My best man Will agreed with others, "Dylan's really coming into his voice."

Sometimes compliments are obvious attempts to cover up a lack of skill. No worries, I had my mom's gift of simple rhyming and used it to spit terrible raps as my alter ego Dyl-Mo-Flo. Rhyming was easy, harmonizing was unattainable.

Singing is interesting. It seems to run in families. Many music acts, from the Avetts to Willie and his sons, share the gene for matching pitch. Even my middle name-sake's son, Jakob Dylan, kept it tight with one head-light from the Wallflowers. Rhyme intended.

I took a few voice lessons while coaching the novice crew shell at Williams College in spring 2006. Finally, the music instructor leveled with me and said, you can work on posture and singing from your belly but in the end, just like musical range, there is a certain amount of potential improvement. I had the singing equivalent of a twelve-inch vertical, and might be able to dunk on an eight-foot rim—with practice.

I could sing Meher Baba's line "Don't worry be happy" with a Jamaican twist in nearly "perfect" pitch. So I happily belted on with the family jam circles into the late night, not worrying too much if I couldn't find the har-mony. In the 'circle game,' a name coined by Mom, friends and family had the choice to perform or request a song from another circlegoer. Ageless guitars and Ugandan djembes were passed round as the night passed by. More rum and eggnog led to the addition of ukuleles, violins, squeeze-box accordions, harmonicas, mandos, musical spoons, egg shakers, random clay trumpets, wood blocks, cymbals, and anything else that could produce a rhythm or tune.

The Moro family room lived well and loudly.

CHAPTER ELEVEN

TOO LEGIT TO QUIT OR DOUBT

Children don't take joy in bringing heartache to their parents. In fact, it is the opposite. As I heard my mother's voice tremble a bit as she explained, I knew I was venturing down a path that might bring up some hard questions and memories for those involved. But selfishly, I felt inclined to push on to truth.

Truth can be subjective, depending on perspective. My ultimate truth may be different than what my parents had deemed as their truth—that I was theirs and they were mine. Our family connection was inherently, completely true. I was theirs. However, the possibility remained and was gaining impetus that my genetic code could potentially be different.

As we waited for Jer's results to be analyzed by the lab, my secondary and thus confirming AncestryDNA results came back. They provided concrete evidence (thus negating my potential denial) that I was about fifty-one percent Jewish.

One difference from the 23andMe results was these latest AncestryDNA provided me with my first real DNA connections, as three strong genetic relatives immediately populated on my newest connections' dashboard. The bat of reality struck me. I knew two of these names very well. They were first cousins on my mother's side I had grown up with throughout my life, two of the cousins in my original group text a month or so earlier that had not responded back.

"First cousin" is the exact distance of relation that Ancestry blindly identified as well. The test was legit.

A third relative was unfamiliar, Janice Wertheimer from New Jersey. Clicking on our connection from a genetic perspective, she was 100 percent Jewish. She showed up for me as a second cousin, one step down the ladder from my known maternal first cousins.

Behind fingers of excitement, I sent my first cousins a message saying something to the effect of, hey, this is so cool you are on here! And by spitting in a tube, without any knowledge of us being cousins, our DNA actually tracked us correctly and this entire thing is accurate.

Wait, I thought, what am I saying? Am I saying if this is legitimate, then the entire thing must be accurate too? Could it be that half of my DNA on my mom's side was correct, but the other half was improperly analyzed? Not likely. In fact, on 23andMe each chromosome is mapped out specifically with the type of DNA being attributed. Think of each gene on each chromosome being a heads or tails flip—mother or father gene—and from there it can be color coded to show the exact nucleotide breakdown. Each chromosome showed multiple colors instead of a complete one-color shade.

Therefore, the idea of only half of my saliva being correctly sampled seemed illogical. Each individual chromosome accurately showed a split of both maternal and paternal coin flip, as opposed to every other chromosome rotating in one complete solid color between a given parent.

In other words, if all of this was accurate, what were the ramifications?

How does one spin a dreidel?

THE DREIDEL SONG OR HOLY NIGHT

This mid-December thirty-seventh anniversary day of celebration for my parents coincided with the start of my own daughter Zuzu's second (and, in reality, first interactive) holiday season. In an email, I was asked if my family celebrated Christmas or Hanukkah (more to come on the email sender later).

It was a strange question to read. In fact, this was the first time in my life I had ever been asked. Keena had been to every Christmas service put on at her small-town Lutheran church, the same church where we had our wedding. During the 2020 global pandemic, Keen had regretfully said the thing she would miss most about the holidays in a time of virtual gatherings would be the in-person candlelight service singing of "Holy Night."

GENERATIONAL RELIGION

Johnny was raised a strict Catholic, even attending Catholic school and serving as an altar boy. He spoke of the hypocrisy within the church and the feeling of being physically disciplined by nuns throughout his formative years. Needless to say, he made a choice to distance from this organized faith, and spoke to us about paying close attention to the words in red in his Bible.

"These were Jesus' words, and the only truth that matters," he would say. "The rest has been translated, transcribed, and subjectively changed."

Debra still valued her Methodist upbringing and would seek out the kind of candlelight services Keen enjoyed. Deb and Johnny never promoted our family as needing to be an every-Sunday churchgoing group. Again, my family's church was "of the outdoors"—wet Pacific Ocean beach walks with cold toes and salty air, and fresh mossy woods walks through old growth stands.

Not once in my holiday history had I considered lighting a menorah. In fact, my only point of reference to Hanukah came thanks to Adam Sandler's classic *SNL* song, which I once learned to strum along with, "Harrison Ford's a quarter Jewish—not too shabby."

Heck, if Han Solo and Indy Jones had some Jewish DNA, maybe I should consider celebrating Hanukkah. Or Matzah Ballin, as read the socks my sister-in-law Tess gifted me during the holidays after my DNA test first came back.

CHAPTER TWELVE

RATIONALIZING COUSIN QUESTIONING IN PRINT

Upon reaching out to my cousins on Ancestry messenger, one wrote back. I think they confused the message thread, having meant the message for our third cousin, but accidentally sending it to me. They wrote, "This is so cool, feel bad for Dylan... he didn't know uncle John wasn't his dad."

Had I been so naive as to not consider this outcome? Of course not, but it was different seeing it in print from someone else, someone who I cared about and cared about me. My defense system was immediately engaged. He's still my dad! Genetics don't determine fatherhood. Fatherhood is a choice, right? Both in momentary act and long-term commitment? The biology of being a dad—are they separate, the same, or indifferent to each other?

The questions started rolling and I settled on a mantra I would use to push forward. Regardless of what my exact story would unfold to be, I was appreciative of who I was and how I had come to be. I was attempting to reconstruct an unknown domino pattern and yet, fundamentally, I would not exist without it.

Back in elementary school, I was "just thankful to be alive," and that self still remained. Be it fate or luck, I was created and I was placed in a loving home with selfless parents who gave me the essentials to Maslow's hierarchy. Food, safety, shelter, and, more importantly, time and love.

From this perspective I could settle in and spin a positive vibe to pursue the unknown question: What was the face in the mirror made of?

The truth I had known for thirty-five years now stood in contradiction with new scientific facts that presented a change in the genealogy coding for the physiology of features. But genealogy does not determine the complete makeup of spirit, personality, or unique entity. My dad was my dad. I was his and he was mine.

DYNAMICS OF MY DAD STEPPING UP

As I've been working through this writing, Johnny sent me this text:

> A little story... I moved to Portland in April of 1980, met your mom and became good friends. About two-and-a-half years later we were intimate, when she told me that she was pregnant and that the baby could be mine, I offered her a place to stay while she was going through her pregnancy. I was almost thirty-two, I had been partly responsible for an abortion when I was younger. When you were born, and I first held you in the warm bath, you were mine and I made a commitment to something I was looking for, a family...there is no doubt in my mind as to who I am, I love you, there's no denying that.

BUT WHY AND FOR WHO?

Many would ask me: Why do you really want to know? What does it do for you? Why would you want to change the course of your known life? Are you not content?

All fair questions. I had three intrinsic motivators for answers. One was the pursuit of scientific fact, the inward adventure. More importantly, what if I have an entire genetic family tree unbeknownst to me, or them (could I be a positive linchpin)? And most importantly, I wanted to be able to tell our future daughter, the one Keen and I had just gotten the best news of our lives about via positive dipstick, her full story to the best of my abilities.

For these reasons I committed to a search. Most evenings I spent on my phone or TV zoning out to some inconsequential info about the latest NBA free agent, the weather forecast for a potential bike or hike, or, even worse, Craigslist car shopping. I could simply repurpose this time and energy into a relentless search.

But for what, or whom?

YOUNG DAYſ

As a child we hung in coffee shops on the Coos coast of Oregon as our parents played originals for small crowds. They would pass out cassettes with a pencil drawing of Johnny sketched by Deb. I was both proud and, as a young person, at times embarrassed of their abilities. My pops would often hit the high falsetto and my mom would find the syncopated harmonies to enhance his sound exponentially more vividly.

Our cozy two-bedroom, modest in size, was bursting with love and togetherness. Most evenings my siblings and I would fall asleep to the piano or acoustic guitar coming from the living room straight back to our bedrooms.

Music doesn't fully pay the bills for most people, especially when kids are pulling up to the table. Johnny became a committed hairstylist, even spending weekends cleaning the salon to pull a little extra coin. My siblings and I would literally pull up cushions in the salon's waiting room couch to find the left-behind coins that had slipped out of customers' pockets. I honed my NBA Jam and Street Fighter II skills one rediscovered quarter at a time in the Pony Village Mall arcade.

My dad gave me a fresh haircut every two weeks, like clockwork. A hair-dried 'bump' was imperative to really pull off the look. I've joked with my pops that he has cut the hair on my head (less and less of it each year) more than any other human in his life. Even as those cuts have slowed down through the years, as we're separated by a thousand miles, give or take, I often hold out on a cut until I get to see him. I appreciate the chance to reconnect and time to visit one on one. He always starts the cut with the same classic Johnny question, "Which one of these hairs do you want cut?"

My response since 2007, "Just give me the Gumuz special."

It's a nod to the shaved look of the group of Ethiopians I'd spent a month with on the Sudanese border while digging a water cistern with my best man Will. My experience there, meeting expat nurses in Africa, led to me pursuing a nursing degree and meeting my classmate and future "wifey of lifey," Keena.

Dad's detailed approach and ability to work with his hands made him a fine hairstylist, a label I found somewhat embarrassing in middle school years.

"You mean your dad cuts hair? But he isn't a barber?"

"Ya, his uncle had a beauty school so he was trained and taught in southern Cali as a stylist."

Dad's squint, as he angles your ears to line up the sideburns, has become exponentially more intense. With Deb coaching him over his shoulder, he continues to make his way through this profession of cutting one's hair—even though his true life's passion would be using his hands for making music and his voice to belt original lyrics instead of carrying on conversations with those under his cape.

He did it for us. To provide income and stability to the family, which continued to grow each few years through the eighties until there were four kids, making him the fifth man and Deb the first sub off the bench. The team played out in the wedding weekend Byrd versus Moro hoops game, a hotly contested 'tie' game.

DEB'S PASSION FOR CAREGIVING

Deb was fortunate to pursue her passion of being a mom at home with kids. She worked various jobs through our growing years, including waitress and grocery store clerk. In fact, we worked together my freshman year of high school summer.

I was saving up for my first car. It would be a well-kept but already aged five-speed 1986 Mercury Lynx, with the hatchback and dashboard maroon carpet. I would fill the ice machines and count cans, and she would let me know what needed mopped, or help me pack out boxes of veggies for the outdoor produce stand. I would strain my back as I threw every pound of my underdeveloped frame into proving I could lift a box of melons out to the front parking lot.

She continued her life's niche of selflessly caring for others as we grew. She provided support to a young man with Lesch Nyhan syndrome, who was all about the fun and experiences a typical early-twenties dude might be into.

This affinity for giving to others eventually morphed into her opening her own in-house daycare, where she and my dad nurtured young kids. My siblings and I would say Deb didn't as much run a daycare as she played as a child, leading other children all day long—typically into exhaustion by the end of the daycare day.

These side gigs, along with Johnny's work as a night-shift youth juvenile officer and bronze foundry slurry room worker, provided enough money for our family to be comfortable. Though the fridge was filled for a few days at a time at most, we had good food prepared by Johnny, who had a passion for cooking. We had modest homes, with enough space to share a room with a sibling but still maintain our own space. We always got to participate in activities, and to get that new bike for a birthday or the Christmas gift we desired.

That being said, things were tight. If an argument was going to happen it was going to revolve around Debra spending more than the budget might allow, or that after our last trip there wouldn't be extra money for the next six-plus months. As a kid, I would cringe with that knot-in-my-stomach feeling as they bantered about cash flow. I thought we were poor, or maybe I knew it, but I also had the perspective to realize there were people in much tougher spots than us, and that money wasn't the only value of equity.

PERSPECTIVE OF VALUE

We were rich in time and love. Our weekends as a family were spent in the church of the outdoors, visiting Shore Acres, rainy cold beaches of the Pacific, hiking in the woods hunting for chanterelle mushroom. Late evenings at my uncle's place we'd share fresh crab and smoked salmon. The adults would sing and play acoustic guitars into the night, kids would pass out wherever they were comfortable.

My cousin's home had a great view of the bay surrounded by forest and ponds with salamanders to explore. Their heavy solid door welcomed you with a classiness brought on by wealth with warmth and fun. My cousin Brando was my hero. He was athletic, adventurous, funny, kind-hearted, and just cool. My memories of spending time with him are vivid—playing Tyson's Punch Out, shooting hoops (hoping the ball didn't roll all the way down the sloped hill), and sleeping over on his waterbed while a Gremlin figurine's glow-in-the-dark eyes stared down at us. A bit creepy, but I felt safe when hanging with Brando. He was like my big brother, and had a positive influence on me that extended beyond his days on earth and remains in my heart today.

Growing up in Oregon in the early nineties, Nike and Jordans were big-time. I was fixated on the brand, and would spot and instantly cast judgments based on what kicks another kid was sporting. Of course, I wasn't wearing the Jordans I dreamed of, but a lot of us weren't. It was usually the kid who had no hoops skills whose parents bought him the goods.

My best buddy's aunt worked for Nike and he got a hookup to Blazers games and gear. He had a Nike cap that I coveted. I'm sure I talked about it constantly, but I don't remember. What I do remember is my mom sewing a Nike swoosh she'd cut out of black felt onto a brand-less gray cap with black bill she had found on clearance. She was skilled, and it was not noticeable to others. Only I knew—and though I had a massive appreciation for her kindness and the perspective that the brand didn't really matter in terms of quality, I still selfishly wanted the real deal. I even cut out the inside tag to hide evidence of the hat's truth.

Through the years we would buy used family vans, and I still remember the pride I would feel when we seemed to upgrade a very basic social status symbol. Even if it was used with a few miles, it was new to us. I inherently put value on stuff, on belongings, a tendency my parents always advised against based on morals of importance. They had to, out of necessity. In my family we placed value on a good homemade meal, a walk in the woods, a great song, or a funny joke.

My parents were never overly motivated to pursue a career or to be defined by a career. In fact, they were proud of the way they chose to live their lives. It was presented as a dichotomy of sorts; either money or time, not both.

POVERTY AND PURPOSE

When I was applying to college at age eighteen, filing the FAFSA was an instant eye opener. I knew my parents were on a shoestring budget. I also knew my pops' credit was flawless. It was a point of pride for him, as he would juggle small amounts of debt between various temporary zero-percent credit cards.

For the federal student aid form, they ask for parental income, and there it was, a family of six and my parents' combined income in 2001 was less than $20,000. It was enough for us. We took trips to see family, and stayed involved in activities that had a participation cost. My parents had even bought a great little family house in Joseph, Oregon, a destination tourist town by summer and sleepy mountain town in winter.

I learned from my parents how to be thrifty, how to balance need versus want, and that it was okay to accept gifts from others and not be too proud (though I still struggle doing this today in comparison to their ability).

Us kids were motivated to take care of our parents financially. We would give small gifts, or make house fixes, or, at the minimum, pay for our own vehicles, gear, and activities. It felt right to help improve day-to-day life for both ourselves and our parents.

These were good lessons. Living this way, in some ways out of necessity, provided motivation for moving toward financial stability. I often felt a sense of duty or responsibility. Later in life I would feel the tendency towards what I arrogantly would call, "parenting my parents."

Maybe, in a certain sense, every young adult feels this way. We rage against the norms that are constructed around our nurtured environment. Think of the trust-afarian whose take-it-easy approach to life is enabled by hardworking and giving parents.

Was I destined to revolt against my parents' approach to "having enough"? Or was there a blueprint inside that would create inner conflict regardless? Perhaps the thought of self-determination is foolish in itself. As one ages, the ability to find patience and acceptance seems destined to dominate the prefrontal cortex, otherwise life gets pretty sour.

CHAPTER THIRTEEN

IMPATIENTLY SQUEEZING ANY INFO

Deb and I talked through what she knew over a few phone conversations, with Johnny even jumping in on one call.

Mom says she first struck up a conversation with a man on a city bus en route to her spiritual enlightenment group, who called themselves the Premies, followers of Prem Rawat, also known as Guru Maharaj Ji. The Premies believed his "knowledge" could enrich one's pathway through life. As Mom talked I, of course, butted in with little questions such as, "Like some creeper dude on public transit?"

No, not like that, she clarified. He was kind and she introduced herself and invited him to come to hear the Guru's knowledge. He obliged.

"Okay, cool, what did he look like? What do you remember about him?"

Well, she said, he looked like Jesus, like the old brown-haired paintings you see in churches from the sixties.

"Okay—was he tall?"

No, she didn't think he was very tall, maybe around the height of my dad. He was older, though, she remembers thinking he was quite a bit older than her.

This prompted me to do some quick mental math. If my mom is sixty-two, give or take, and he's older, this dude could be pushing his mid-seventies to early eighties.

"Fair enough. What else do you remember?"

He was gentle and kind, she said. It wasn't like he was homeless, but she didn't think he really had a place to live permanently. Like, he wasn't dirty or anything, he just seemed like a traveler who wasn't in one place very long.

"Okay, cool, do you have a name?"

They went by first names, she explained. She was "Debbie," her friend was "Trish," and all she remembered was he went by "Ruhi."

I pressed her, as I often do. I knew this was a fragile situation and I didn't want to bring pain, but I also was staying true to honesty. I knew if we continued to have a relationship based in honesty throughout our lives, we would maintain an unbreakable bond.

"So, like, you don't remember his name, or where he was from, or anything?"

She had a book of poems he gave her. She could see it in her mind, it was a typed, personal paperback called *Petals of Light*. She thought this poetry book might have all the answers we needed. Doubtful, I thought. But okay.

"Any other memories? He must have shared some family history, or where he was from or something, anything?"

She thought he was traveling from maybe Nebraska or something, but his family might have been from the East Coast.

"I'm sorry, Dylan," she said, with a tremble in her voice. " I don't remember the details. We did not have a relationship like that."

I kept pushing, "Surely you have some sort of name?"

She remembered thinking he had two first names, like Lawrence and Martin. Great, I thought, my best clue is Martin Lawrence.

"Was he Jewish? Did he look like me at all or anything?"

He looked like Jesus, she repeated. It was hard to say, he'd be much older now. In fact, she believed, he'd passed away.

ACTION REACTION

I had attempted to compartmentalize my emotions behind my mantra of *I wouldn't change anything, for my life would not be as it is*, but now my resolve started to sputter. This new information felt like a ton of bricks to the dome. How could this work?

I find out after thirty-five years that I may not have the genes of my pops? I have no name for the potential biological dude, who very well is already dead? What can a search help solve?

Some might say this scenario could actually be better than the alternatives. His potential death and the lack of clues to connect could serve as an easy out, provided I had the good grace to simply leave it alone. Find the rug, find the broom, and do what one does. The cousins hadn't responded anyway. If mum was the word, I could play along, right?

I couldn't, it wasn't me. I pressed Mom.

"How do you know he is dead?"

Her friend who was part of the Premie group told her, she said, but she's probably passed as well by now.

Now, feeling a sense of dissension and lacking respectful tact, I go, "Oh, really? How do you know she is dead and what is her name?"

Her name was Trish, she said, and she was Mom's friend when she was pregnant with me. Mom worked for her sewing part time. She lived in Portland, but Mom thought she passed years ago. She was elderly then and would be so old now.

"Okay, well let me check into it," I said. A quick Google search (as I became argumentatively addicted to over the course of this journey) with her name and Portland, Oregon, and I had a phone number.

Boldness has never been a fear factor of mine, so once I got off the phone with my mom, I immediately placed a cold call to Trish, explaining my situation. I jumped in directly so as to not come off as some telemarketer fumbling through a random sales pitch. I started in a fashion that would become my temporary norm.

"Hi, my name is Dylan Moro and this is super random, but I am hoping to track down a man that I believe may be my biological father, and I think you may have some information that could potentially help, Debbie Brink is my mother."

I would put it all out in a long, run-on, one-breath sentence so she, and later others, might not have time to interject or hang up. I feared rejection like a young college dude asking a crush out for the first time.

The voice on the other side was kind and genuine. "Oh, Debbie, how is she? Is she doing well?" We shared a short catch-up, I gave her my mom's phone number, and said that I would be in touch.

Immediately, I called my mom back and told her, gloating somewhat, "I found your friend. She is still alive and lives in the same home in Portland. I gave her your contact, she was happy to hear about you and would love to reconnect. She didn't know of a man named 'Ruhi,' but said she would call around to her other Premie friends and see if anyone else might have a contact."

I went on. "So now that she is still alive, what made you think or say that she was dead? And if she was the one who told you about 'Ruhi,' how do you then know that he is dead?"

"They were just older, Dylan, so I am just thinking they have already probably passed," she said. "I feel like someone told me that he had, but maybe I am wrong."

"Do you remember anything else, mom, anything at all?" I said, taking on an annoying role as a pseudo-lawyer approaching the bench.

Not really, she said. Like she said before, she seemed to remember him having two first names for a full name, like maybe Lawrence something, or like Martin Lawrence, but she could just be confused on that now.

"I don't remember his name, I'm sorry."

I knew I had pressed enough and needed to let emotions simmer a bit.

"It's okay, Mom, thanks for sharing what you do remember. It's cool that your friend is still alive and would like to visit with you."

"Ya that is nice," she said. "Listen, Dylan, I love you, and I am here to help in any way that I can, and let's go down this path together if you wish."

And then she launched into the story. The story of how I was conceived.

"I was living with Uncle Gary on the coast in North Bend taking care of your cousins while they worked and went to school. Ruhi came down to visit one weekend. I think he must have taken the bus down," she started. "He would call me sometimes and was always gentle and kind. I want you to know that, it's not like he was a bad guy or something. Anyway, he came to visit and we borrowed Uncle Gary's black Desoto and went to the beach. I just remember that he really liked me and we were intimate just that night.

The week before, for the first and only time, your dad, John, and I also were close for a night. I had not had a partner in five years, and then within a week I had two partners.

I didn't know how to feel about it, but I loved your dad, and when he asked me to move back in with him and we decided to raise you, my prayers were answered. And my life has been exactly what I always dreamed of from that moment on. Because of you, we fell in love and made a family and had all of your siblings, because of you.

We knew you were ours, you had blue eyes like Grandma Nana."

It was difficult to hear, and a tad cringeworthy, but also, we had a trust that allowed it to flow. I continued to press, "Thanks for being honest, mom, but you must have known there was potential that I could have been his child."

What a weird sentence to say, or even still write.

"No, Dylan, you must understand," she said, and here for the first time she expressed some firmness. "You were ours, mine and your dad John's, that was all that mattered to us."

THE MIND WARP
OF A NEW REALITY

Fair enough, I thought, but then I flipped to a new question—what about Ruhi? Did he ever follow up? Was it truly fair to not give him the opportunity to know his son, to deprive him of this knowledge?

By casting this stone into the pond of finding the truth, there would be a ripple effect. I could start to make it out. How would Johnny feel about this? Oh, no prob, I rationalized, he would be cool and understanding. Remember, at his core he's easygoing and loves me. Plus, he must have had some idea, too, right?

What position am I putting my mom in? Indirectly or directly, it forces her to reopen a part of her life that she had chosen to close off and, unfortunately, in our society women seem to be judged by a different standard than men when it comes to close relationships.

Jerri, Julian, Lena—will they feel duped by this? Will it affect our relationships? Again, I rationalized. No, we're cool, it doesn't change that they are my siblings. It just might shed light on some physical variations and maybe even personality differences.

What a strange thought—in light of this potential knowledge, am I now someone different? In other words, do I have innate personality traits as well? This seemed heavy, so I mentally tabled the thought and vowed to revisit.

How about my wife Keena, and future daughter Zuzu? Well, Keena knows me best. She loves and is frustrated by my energy and perpetual motion, my unrelenting lack of idle contentment. She would support me no matter what and do what she does best—keep me balanced.

How about extended family and friends, would they cast judgment? I wasn't so worried about myself, but I worried about my parents, specifically my mom. She didn't do anything wrong. It's not unheard of for a person to get a knock at the door from a seeming stranger greeting them with a vital story of past history. Think of men who were unaware of having fathered children, or biological mothers who put a child up for adoption.

I wasn't worried about judgment. In fact, I felt more of an excitement. I liked that I had a potentially unique story. Sure, it was muddled and muddy at the time, but this was a possible adventure that I could share with others. My longtime nuclear family may have a different tree trunk than previously known. My mom and dad had given me unrelenting confidence, and this journey was not going to shake that, but I wanted Zu to know. So as far as I was concerned, either everyone else could get on board, or no worries—my daughter was of much greater importance.

Finally, what about this Ruhi character, the traveling poet? I had been feeling a need to at least inform him of my existence, knowing he could do with that information as he wished. That feeling was cemented when my mom told me she thought he tried to contact her later in the fall of 1982, when she had moved back in with my dad. At that time, it was made clear to him that Debra was moving on, and so should he.

That was the story that made me feel a great deal of empathy and sadness for him. I put myself in his shoes, a guy who may have loved a lady and then was never allowed to reconnect or even know that he may have a child. It seemed unfair. It gave me new motivation.

CHAPTER FOURTEEN

MY LIFE A TIPPING POINT

Meanwhile I continued my journey of research. As I had done on my mom's side with the cousins group chat, I also reached out to my dad's relatives to see if any of them had taken a genetic test.

My Uncle Jimmy, Johnny's elder bro, had in fact done a test. In the group chat with my pops' fam, he screen-shotted and shared his dashboard from Ancestry.com. At this point my second confirmation sample from Ancestry had not been fully processed yet, but the genetic dominos continued to fall. His genetic makeup showed dominance in Italian, Spanish, and Native American, compared to my initial sample from the competitor company 23andMe reporting no such groups. Denial was becoming more and more futile.

His sister must have questioned his action of sharing of the genetic info, because under his screenshots he wrote, "What, he's an adult, he deserves to know the truth."

This was a powerful thing to read. I started to have a feeling that perhaps I was at the naive center of a story for which the others already had the script.

Maybe this was why my mom's family had ghosted me in response. Perhaps they knew, and yet didn't want to be the bearer of the burden of reality. Instead of reality falling like dominoes, perhaps it was more like a boulder of truth that had already fallen before my awareness. The boulder had been replanted back on top of a cliff and excruciatingly, gingerly propped up with minimal balance, awaiting the right amount of wind or rain to send it crashing down to reveal the truth below. My life; a tipping point.

The question was, where was I positioned? Was I behind the boulder, pushing? And in what direction—uphill or down? Or was I at the bottom of the cliff, awaiting my inevitable flattening, a la Wile E. Coyote and Road Runner?

But I was aware of the deal. Very few people forty years ago foresaw the day that someone could order a small cardboard box with a smaller plastic vial, fill it with a few cc's of saliva, place it back in the mail, and send it to a lab where it would be extracted, analyzed, genetically mapped, and linked to stored samples that could be compared; thus, connecting one to his or her genetic location of origin and genetic family members. In other words, even sci-fi movies of the early eighties, which my pops loved and nurtured us into becoming aficionados of, weren't touching on how easy genetic identification might be in the near future. In fact, my reality was proof that this science would be commonplace within only one generation.

I couldn't negate my parents' understanding of their own truth. The question was whether or not I was justified in demanding this knowledge as an adult, if I deserved to know something that had not so much been held from me but, more so, had been presented as a positive connector versus a potential divider.

It was a paradox. It was my life after all, but it was a selfish act I was pursuing. I was uncovering other selfish decisions—or selfless decisions, depending on one's perspective—that could set truth free and, at the same time, bring potential pain to those I loved and who loved me.

HE'S ALWAYS BEEN AND WILL BE A MORO

Over the holidays a few months later, my Aunt Tina, who had questioned Uncle Jimmy's revealing of this info, told Keena with tears in her eyes, "He's a Moro, that's all that matters, and he will always be a Moro."

They were standing in the famous Moro kitchen, which for years had pumped out the greatest Italian/Mexican dishes for miles around. Sometimes the sweetest words and sentiments come from the most surprising of places.

For years, I had felt a bit of a strange comparison and competition with Tina's only son, Jeremy, my elder cousin by half a year. He grew up living with our grandparents, and seemed like a Moro through and through. His inherent connection with my grandparents, justified by his need for them (they served in many ways as his stable caregivers) could never be matched, so I needed not try. He made some bad choices growing up, but during the summer of '97, when Jer and I stayed with them, Jeremy always looked out for me and treated me with great respect and pride.

When we were little and my Uncle Jimmy had a wedding, Jer and Jeremy were chosen to be part of the bridal party, flower girl and ring bearer respectively. My minimal memories of the event could be based simply on past photos, but I vividly remember them getting to roll in in a blow-your-mind limo. I also remember the numbing feeling of acceptance, or perhaps lack of acceptance, of putting on display what Dwight Schrute would call the "money beets", with their olive skin and familiar looks, while pushing to the side my somewhat lighter eyes, hair, and skin.

Of course, now as an adult I can see this is silly. They simply needed a little dude and little lady to help fill out their wedding party and, by selecting a nephew and niece from two siblings, they helped to share and spread the love. Also Jimmy had functioned as Jeremy's male role model, in a certain sense, by helping to coach his youth baseball teams while attempting to provide positive direction, which at times was a challenge for all members of the family.

Anyway, while all of these feelings could be deposited in the box of simple youth jealousy, I nonetheless have always had a small sentiment of being a bit different.

At the end of the day, when we were rolling north back to Oregon after a week's holiday vacation in sunny southern Cal, I had my pops and mom in the front and siblings crashed out on blankets in the back of our blue, carpeted-ceiling Econoline van. Jeremy had a tough empty hole stemming from his lack of a stable father figure. Grandpa Moro, Uncle Jimmy, and older twin cousins all attempted to partially plug the hole, but quantity can never surpass quality. So, I felt empathy for him and appreciative of my "nuclear family."

Regardless of what truth I might fully uncover with my pops, he had been my "rock and role model" for being a good dude. He showed me how to approach life with ample and unconditional love, sometimes tough, but always present.

FAMILY ON THE MOVE

Immediately following my fourth-grade school year, my parents decided to move the family from the rainy coast and find a new home in the mountains. For the next few months we camped as a family all over Oregon, Idaho, Washington, and Northern California. We went with the minimal and cheap route of tent camping. We would share one big family tent, taking turns telling funny and scary stories we made up on the spot, before falling asleep in the cool mountain air. It was an adventure and exciting to think what might be next for our family.

We were each other's stability. Flexible acceptance was the name of the game as my parents saved and planned for the move back to the Wallowa Mountains of Oregon for my high school years. At an auction, my dad made a last-second bid to win a rundown house for $2,500 in my mom's hometown of Plankinton, South Dakota, which landed us living in the Midwest for the next four years.

Our years in the lower Dakota were great, with ample family time and freedom to bike through our small town all summer long. We felt safe living in a place where everyone knew everyone. As fate would have it, the auctioned and fixed-up "Plank house" would be in my family's hands when I was looking at going back to nursing school post-Africa travels. My mom, as a casual suggestion, thought that Dakota Wesleyan University in neighboring Mitchell, South Dakota, might have a nursing school. Sure enough, they had not only a strong program but a spot opening as of that Monday morning. If I could make it out, I would start the following Monday.

So, my bro Julio and I rolled back east to SoDak, fresh with five-gallon jugs of filtered, used veggie oil, loaded the '76 Mercedes 300D "Blue Bonnet grease car" gifted to me by my cousin. Using a conversion kit from a company called Greasecar, I had converted the car's diesel engine to run off used vegetable oil from local restaurants. I'd worked with a local mechanic, Peter, on the conversion. Peter was a first-generation German immigrant with a thick German accent and a love for Mercedes vehicles. We took to each other immediately, bonding over my maternal German heritage.

KEENS

A few months later, a cute little nursing student from the Badlands of South Dakota was willing to humor my unrelenting trash talk as she officiated the sand volleyball rec game I was disgracing with my poor skills.

Suddenly, my life would have purpose and direction, as I stumbled through telling her outside George McGovern's campus library. "If we start this, then I don't see how it can end. I wouldn't be able to hurt you like that, because it would hurt me too much."

Maybe this was my new insight into what love was, or maybe I just selfishly realized she made me a better dude. Three years later, at the altar, I cornily changed lyrics to our favorite Jack Johnson song and heard back the most genuine and original words of love and commitment from Keen. I didn't deserve her.

Her pops Harvey might have jokingly agreed. It took three attempts to ask for his blessing for her hand. Third time's the charm. Down on one knee at her parents' green-and-gold Packers house on Christmas morn, I asked, "If it's okay with you now, Harve, I was going to ask your daughter if she'd marry me?"

With a tear in his eye, he gave me the head nod. Her brother was just "flabbergasted," and her entire family was so loving and kind to accept all of my ridiculous humor and constant bombardment of energy.

Keen brought a balance, toughness, and commonsense approach to help me navigate this world. At a young age she seized a nurturing role of responsibility for her siblings—we were both the eldest of four—and she provided the same to me. I fell in love with how much she cared about her family, and I was inspired by the Byrds' unmatched closeness and how they prioritized time together. It felt familiar, as well. I felt a similar bond with my fam. Witnessing the Byrds and the Moros building friendships on the basketball court, over a meal, or on shared vacations has been one of my greatest joys in life.

Keen embodies hard and unconditional love. She went from nearly failing intro nursing chem, thus being booted from the program, to being the top nursing student two years later and eventually completing her doctorate.

The care that she, her mother, and siblings showed for their terminally ill father was inspirational. She continues to commit her life towards humbly serving others, only hoping in return for some quick time to run and share time with Zu. She puts up with me, guides me, supports me, and sometimes even thinks I am funny. My life would be devoid without her and Zu.

In naming our first-born Keen proposed Zuzu Byrd Moro, and I was happy to oblige. The Byrd pays tribute to Keen's father, Harvey Byrd, who she and her family lost in 2016 after a courageous battle with Lewy Body Dementia. I had no second thought of sharing my known last name with our daughter. In giving our daughter Byrd Moro we were continuing our family's lineages.

CHAPTER FIFTEEN

THE RABBIT HOLE
OF ROLES AND BIRDS

The scale was tipping more and more toward the inevitable need to accept the truth—my dad, the man who raised me from birth until now, was not my biological father. His genetics did not code for my new cells.

On one hand, it felt like I was an imposter. It felt like half of my genes were being changed by an unknown source, a sort of genetic parasitism. For thirty-five years, the genes had been able to hide out and mask themselves as close enough or similar enough to not be noticed, at least from my naive perspective. But now, the genetic lineage that I was passing on to my unborn daughter was unknown to me as well.

I was experiencing a strange dichotomy between feeling like a placeholder for a complete stranger's code that was now knowingly infiltrating my own, and yet, at the same time, understanding that the code itself helped to determine who I was and physically what I was made up of.

I had the mental video of David Attenborough's *Life* scene highlighting the cuckoo bird, and could hear him narrating the cringeworthy scene. A mother hen has laid an egg in an unsuspecting host's nest, and now the parasitic brood imposter's egg begins to crack. Upon hatching, the chick is already physically purposed with the genetic gifts to be able to hoist a native egg out of the nest to reserve all food resources for itself. The chick relies on its perfectly shaped back, wings that can be pinned back, and an appropriate amount of strength and dexterity to then extend its legs and hoist the other eggs out of the nest. This imposter chick sends the other, competitive and rightful, eggs to their inevitable demise before they are even given the opportunity to fight for survival.

Gravity is not kind on free-falling eggs, and nature is not kind on genetically weaker breeds or individuals. The creepiness escalates when the cuckoo becomes dominant not just in the physical realm, but genetically superior in the mental realm. In her confusion, the blinded mother host bird continues to feed the cuckoo fledgling as it grows to be her physical superior.

Watching the video of the chick's mouth wide open, demanding nurturing and nourishment that seems unjust, I had felt skin-crawling betrayal. Was I the host mother and my genes the cuckoo? Was I lacking the self-awareness to be able to look in the mirror and see the reality? Then again, is it really the mother bird's fault if she lacks the genes to allow for pheromonic or physical recognition of what her real chicks should have looked like, smelt like, sounded like?

Heck, they were never even born to have the moment of imprinting on one another. The mother was naïve, only understanding the data being presented. I could understand this and sympathize with her now more than ever. Furthermore, the parasite cuckoo has developed the genetic traits to allow and exploit such a loophole. Is this not so much different than a CEO demanding workers to provide hours upon hours to produce a product the CEO benefits from? One striking difference: compensation.

Which made me consider looking closer at the host mother bird. Did the parasite imprint on her in such a way that she felt love for this chick, regardless of genetic code, even if in fact the imposter was doing the most terrible acts to her genetics...ending them? This chick was murdering the uncracked lives within the shells she had worked to grow, feed, produce, protect, and build a nest for.

Furthermore, the parasite chick then was taking all resources the host-mother could provide and turning her laborious efforts and literal remaining days of life into feeding itself, and thus enabling its genetics to be passed on by taking advantage of the next unsuspecting preyed-upon nest.

Perhaps I wasn't the mother bird, but instead the parasitic chick, and Johnny was the mother bird. What place did this put Deb in? Yes, a creepy rabbit hole probably not worth diving into too deep (the movie *Vivarium* takes the dark plunge). Did the lack of knowledge liberate me from wrong-doings? In other words, was naivety an out?

Was this Ruhi character actually the cuckoo, and we were all playing willing or unwilling hosts in our own way?

I think all of these scenarios are inaccurate.

The facts: my mom and dad were close. My mom got pregnant. They made a choice to raise me as theirs together. I was born and we all imprinted on each other. My parents fell into a deeper love. Three more children were born out of this love. They have just celebrated thirty-seven years of happy and challenging marriage, but they remain together and in love with each other, their kids, their kids' partners, their additional daycare and exchange student pseudo kids, and their grandchildren.

Humans don't seem as cold or simply "out for survival" as living organisms in nature—however sometimes situations arise in which they can be.

DAD LOVE

My pops, Johnny, made a choice to love me as his own son regardless of what precipitated my mother's pregnancy. Perhaps they both knew there was a potential my genes came from a third party, but it did not ultimately matter to them, for I was theirs to nurture, and they were willing and driven to go forth together.

I have a great appreciation for my dad. As my maternal Grandma Lena put it when I shared with her about my newly discovered genetics, "John loved you. He made his life about you and your mom and your siblings."

She also considered his feelings, asking, "How does your dad feel about all of this?"

Here I reapplied my token answer of he's all good, he's open and accepting so it's not a major deal. My defensive and denial sides came out, too. It doesn't matter anyway, he's my dad.

The truth was a little more gray. Sitting next to my parents on my couch in the basement, just the three of us for the first time since getting the genetic results, we started a gentle conversation, with tact, about what this means for all of us. We had similar talks before, over the phone, but this was the first time all three of us talked in each other's company.

At some point my dad asked something to the effect of, what made you want to do this? My answer was simple. I was interested in the science of where we truly came from—were we Aztec Indian, how much German did I have, etcetera? He followed with, well, he would have been fine never knowing, in fact he wished he didn't know.

My immediate reaction was anger. I was thinking, I didn't have a choice to know or not know, or the luxury of not knowing, or even the duality of understanding what trap of truth I might have been stepping into. I was deprived of knowledge, regardless of the intent. Others seemed to know more than I did about my own life, while I was in the dark, and for what reasons?

I wasn't in the wrong here. My parents knew the potential of this situation, but chose to believe their own, self-created truth.

I was without choice. I was simply born and raised with facts that were presented to me. I trusted with my entire heart that my story was exactly as I had been led to believe—blind faith.

But as I settled in, and with help from my mom in explaining, his reaction made more sense. What my dad was really saying was that he wanted me to be his, and his and my mom's alone. He would accept the reality, whatever it might be, but there was a reason he had joked that, hey, maybe he was Jewish, or how accurate are those tests really? He was grasping for a flotation device as we were all sinking into the inevitable reality.

I had taken away their truth, the pact they had made thirty-five years previously, when I was a stick floating in the bathtub. When one believes with all of their heart and conviction in something, who is to say it can't be true? When he saw my blue eyes, perhaps he was looking for any indication that I could be his and his alone. That, ultimately, was what he wanted. If he could see, physically, something that he already felt insurmountably within, what was wrong with that?

I had robbed them of the choice that they had made together, and now my expectation was for them to just jump in and roll with it. How could they have fully informed me of my potential reality without shifting the very foundation we had built our lives together upon? In the end, it doesn't matter. Or does it?

This was the fear I could hear in Jer's voice when I initially called her after getting my results back in the fall. She immediately was thinking of the ramifications, the ripples this may cause in the family's feelings and emotions. Heck, she may have already been experiencing them.

I, however, was selfishly thinking of the potential adventurous journey of finding my Jewish roots, with a healthy amount of skepticism that this entire thing was even real or plausible. It was sort of a joke to me, and I was masking the very serious undertones because I lacked the ability to weigh the entire gravity of the situation. Perhaps it was the Moro in her that intrinsically knew to protect or empathize with our dad. And maybe it was the genetically predisposed lack of empathy within me that didn't quite get it...yet.

CHAPTER SIXTEEN

SIBLINGƧ REƧULTƧ

Jerri's results came back and marched out exactly as we had anticipated: Spanish (19.4%), Italian (14.7%), Broadly Southern European (7.5%), and Native American (7.6%). She even had a hint of African (.7% Congolese and Southern East African Angolan and Northern West Asian, Iranian, Caucasian and Mesopotamian) and Asian (.4% Broadly Chinese and Southeast Asian, Southern India and Sri Lankan), none of which my DNA showed.

We did, however, share the broadly Northwestern European Germanic European genetics that made up about half of each of our code (Jer 46.9% to my 51.3%). Jer also showed a "hair" of Ashkenazi Jewish (0.3% to my 48.7%), so my original theory about my maternal grandmother Lena or my pops Johnny having some Jewish DNA wasn't completely off kilter. Just 99.7% inaccurate. As Adam Sandler might say, not too shabby.

Just as all humans, both of us are made up of the same basic six elements in atomic form—carbon, hydrogen, nitrogen, oxygen, phosphorus, and sulfur or, as I teach my current sixth grade students, SCHNOPS.

Years later, my bro Julio would submit his 23andMe sample as well. He showed Northwestern European (French and German 57% to my 51.3%) and Southern European (31.3% to my 0%), and more specifically Italian (19.2% to my 0%), Spanish, and Portuguese (6.3% vs 0%), Greek and Balkan (.5% to 0%), Broadly Southern European (5.3% to 0%).

Julio, just like Jer, had a fingernail 0.3% Ashkenazi Jewish, 5.4% Native American, Western Asian, and North African (4.0%); of which Arab, Egyptian and Levantine (1.2%), Iranian Caucasian and Mesopotamian (.9%), North African (.2%), Broadly Western Asian and North African (1.7%), South Asian Southern Indian and Sri Lankan (.2%).

More importantly, though, when their results came back both my siblings were linked to me as a half-sister (25.2% DNA shared) and a half-brother (28.3% DNA shared). It was confirmed, the science was there. The blurring of committed faith and one's truth had been sealed into fact. It continued to amaze me that on a planet with a human population nearing eight billion, without any research or tangible personal knowledge, a company could take saliva, extract DNA, and link half siblings together to a "T."

Later my youngest sister Lena's test was in the same vein as Jer's and Julio's. On the main DNA Relatives dashboard under her name 23.1% DNA shared-Half Sister-Mother's Side. Above Lena's name was Debra Moro, mother, 50.0% DNA Shared, having since also submitted a saliva sample.

People's lives as they knew them were being changed by taking these DNA tests. Whether they were being changed for the better or for the worse, that was in the eye of the beholder. It has long been held that science merely presents truths and facts (albeit perpetually changing truths and facts), and it is up to humans to choose what to do with this information. For me, I was going to start a search. It wasn't necessarily a conscious choice. I was just inherently driven to start the adventure toward closure—or, at least, a greater understanding.

THE WAY TO FIND
THE MISSING SOMETHING
IS TO FIND OUT WHERE IT'S NOT

The first step in this search was to start with the two main leads that had already been presented. My major roadblock in the search was that I did not have a name. I did have a Jewish family member who showed up on Ancestry as a second cousin, Janice Wertheimer.

Ancestry.com measures relationships in terms of a unit called centi-Morgans, cM. It's a unit of recombinant frequency used to measure genetic distance across twenty-one segments of DNA. According to our results, Janice Wertheimer and I shared 440 cM. For the sake of reference, the maternal first cousins I had messaged earlier shared 933 cMs and 804 cMs with me, respectively. So, in essence, this woman Janice was about half as close genetically as my known first cousins.

Simple genetics helped me to theorize that, based on her cMs and her age, late sixties, she was most likely this "Ruhi" character's first cousin. She was 100 percent Ashkenazi Jewish, representing the purity found within Jewish culture.

As I had researched, many Jewish people promoted marriage to other Jews. This led to clean splits marching out 100 percent, 50 percent, 25 percent, 12.5 percent Jewish DNA, depending on the generational split from procreating with another genetically pure Jew. This was also what allowed for the manifestation of some rare genetically linked diseases, such as Tay Sachs.

The other piece of information shown on Janice's dashboard was that she had been an Ancestry member since May 16, 2017, but had not logged on in over a year. In other words, it's entirely possible she activated her membership, checked her sample when it processed, and had never been back on Ancestry since.

Ancestry does not provide any more information than users willingly publish, which typically includes pieced-together family trees. Ancestry customers have the option to create a family tree that they can connect back as many generations as possible, and they can make it either public or private. I had created a very bare-bones tree when I first activated my account, going back just beyond my grandparents' generation with family names to piece together my historical family tree. Ancestry then provided hints based on Census reports and birth, death, and marriage certificates that connect names and locations.

Already, within weeks of ascertaining my genetic sample, my tree was outdated. The hints from certificates and Census reports I was getting on the paternal family names I had listed, Moro and Olivas, were interesting, but inaccurate. And, more importantly, they did nothing to help me in my new pursuit of finding Ruhi.

I immediately cold messaged Janice over the Ancestry app. I sent her a request that I would frequently use, with varying degrees of rewording, over the next two years:

> Hi Janice, my name is John Dylan Moro. I am trying to track down who I believe to be my blood father. He lived in Portland, Oregon, in the early eighties and went by the nickname "Ruhi." I believe him to be of full Jewish DNA, as my result is 50% both on ancestry and 23andme and my mother does not have any Jewish DNA. Anyway, you are my closest genetic relative that is not on my mother's side, so potentially on his, and I just wanted to reach out to see if you may be able to help me connect the dots at all. I appreciate your time; my cell is 541 908 3039 if you would rather call or text. Take care, Dylan Moro

The date of my first message was October 15, 2018. The time was 7:33 p.m. I waited patiently for months—nope, not months, days. Okay, maybe slightly less than a day. The second message was October 16, 2018 at 3:31 p.m.:

> Hi, just wanted to be sure the last message went through? Thanks.

My ever-pervading patience and lack of hyper motivated push, push, pushing was fully on display and engaged. Or perhaps the opposite. My mental calculator was already doing the math. Two unanswered messages plus one year of not logging on equals time for plan B. So again, waiting a healthy twenty minutes with no response, I moved on to the next reasonable research tactic humans did in 2018. I did a Google search, leading to soft-stalking on Facebook.

I say "soft" because I wasn't using Facebook as a tool to peer in and cast judgment. No, in fact, it was just meant as a tool to potentially connect and have a conversation. Fortunately, there was only one Janice Wertheimer on Facebook with this name spelling, and she fit the profile. She was a grandmother from Jersey in her late sixties, early seventies, and based on her Hanukkah postings, she appeared Jewish. She had beautiful grandchildren (see, positive judgment) and, like me, was in education. She was a real person, and I was smothered with the feeling of needing to use delicate tact. So, perhaps not a random Facebook posting.

Heck, I was terrible at the F-book. Keen's sister Brook had just showed me how to use Facebook, and that was just for the purpose of finding potential relatives. I had deleted my lone profile back in 2006 when it was only available for college students. Brook told me, "Dude, it's going to look weird if someone gets a message from you if you don't have any friends or postings, they're going to immediately think you are a creeper or a fake account."

Side note. Back at Oregon State, and racing crew at nationals in Jersey, we had lined up next to the twin rowers from Harvard who later sued Zuckerberg for stealing their "idea" for the original judgment casting app, essentially a digital online yearbook. Side, side note, Zuckerberg, is that a Jewish name? Suddenly anyone Jewish, from Seth Rogen to Andy Samberg, might be a distant relative in my warped mind.

So, I Googled what I knew. I typed in the name Janice Wertheimer and her town in New Jersey, and I found three phone numbers. I looked at it for a few seconds and, without hesitation, picked up the phone and cold called. I immediately jumped in, as I had with Trish, Deb's Portland friend. A man answered.

"Hi my name is Dylan Moro, this is super random, but I am attempting to track down a man that I believe may be my biological father and I think a lady named Janice may be a relative of mine and possible cousin of this man, who goes by," and here I got a bit sheepish, "Ruhi."

A brief pause on the other end, and simply, "Ya, I don't know that name. My wife is Janice, and she wouldn't know that name either. Sorry, goodbye."

Before I could interject, he hung up. The emotions I'd felt building, hope or potential, like a volcano's magma plug, cooled then immediately froze. I was left in solo isolation. I tried the other two numbers, after taking a little pause, just in case, with more tempered expectations, but both had the familiar lady's voice from my childhood telling me "the number had been disconnected and was no longer in service."

Familiarity with one's voice is interesting. We are born with the innate ability for audible recognition as opposed to facial recognition, for which one needs a visual reference point. Another person could recognize a person by their voice without vision involved at all—think younglings in nature that imprint on each other with sound, like sea lions and other pinnipeds. Could there be something instinctive within me to be able to potentially recognize this Ruhi's voice? What about his face or other physical attributes? Was there a type of code that I could crack, if given the opportunity? It seemed highly unlikely.

I needed hard science, and science was hard when my closest potential Jewish relative was either not interested in talking, not willing, or I just flat out had the wrong Janice. Regardless, I went back to the F-book and, my competitive nature coming out, not only cold messaged Janice but also posted the same message on public threads of her previous postings. At the time, this seemed like the only thing I could do. She had not accepted my friend request, so I didn't think I could send a private message. I also thought if there was a sense of a bigger community reading my pleading request for aid, she might feel more compelled and inclined to respond, which she ultimately did.

I used a similar sentiment to the message I had sent over Ancestry's messenger, adding the phrase, "if you are the Janice that submitted and used Ancestry.com about a year ago..." Not getting immediate reply, my restlessness again took over. This had become an ongoing theme, as I attempted to exhaust all options in pursuit. I messaged a handful of people who had been active on her Facebook page, commenting on pictures or linking themselves to her. Most shared the same surname, and I believed them to be her children. Replies received from extended family members: none.

Then, a notification that I had a response to one my threads from Janice. As a Facebook novice, I was excited to learn I would be updated whenever someone posted to me. Ancestry did not function this way when a new message was received, hence my previous immediate follow-up over the Ancestry messenger—or, at least, that is how I rationalized it.

Janice simply stated that she was sorry she couldn't help me, she was not the Janice I was looking for (a sentiment that later would be repeated by others). How could this be? I irrationally attempted to reconcile her statement with my logic. How many Janices with her surname are there who are also Jewish and around the appropriate age?

Maybe she was right. Now, I was probably freaking her out a bit, especially if all of my probes were conspiring together. Husband says, ya some weird dude called me the other day. Daughter says, ya and he popped up on my Facebook, son says, ya me too. And mother attempts to respectfully end this stalking that has now moved from the "soft" realm into the uncomfortable.

I had to pump the brakes a bit.

And yet, I simply didn't believe her or her husband. Might it be that if this dude Ruhi was a wanderer, that he was ostracized by his family? Could his blood relatives have written him off? Was he the black sheep, and I the unbeknownst potential biological son of such a figure?

Putting myself in her shoes, all of the sudden, I might not want to connect either.

QUERY RAMIFICATIONS AND DOCUMENTATION

I had to revamp my approach and consider the ramifications of my query.

I mean, within my own family there were already rocks or even boulders being overturned. I had no idea the full gravity of what impacts I may or may not be making to the potential genetically linked family members who perhaps wanted to unlink for a justifiable reason.

Jer's husband Greg had a childhood buddy who was adopted and later randomly found out that his blood father was Jewish as well (a trend or just a strange coincidence?). Anyway, this buddy, who was about my age and had gone through his search just a few years earlier, had possessed his biological father's full name and location and was able to track him down. He found out that his father had an affair while in Vegas. He had a completely separate family that was not overjoyed to learn of the buddy's existence. In fact, the family had disconnected with the biological father, who was now living solo on a houseboat, I believe, and not very likeable. After all that, the positives were that Greg's buddy had a great childhood with loving adoptive parents, and it seemed that his life was enriched by having been adopted versus having been raised by one or both of his bio parents.

So, needless to say, I needed to keep perspective, tread lightly, and prepare for some potential darkness. Life isn't always the *20/20* special from the nineties. You know, twins separated at birth who married ladies of the same name, have the same job, and both enjoy completing crossword puzzles backwards, go through four toothpicks a day in both earwax picking and tooth prodding, and now that they are reconnected instantly finish each other's sentences, feeling like they have their "besty for esty."

If my gut was correct on Janice, there may be a very purposeful reason as to why she was not rushing to connect or help me out. Then again, also strange that she did the Ancestry DNA test in the first place if there was a real tragic family secret. All that being said, Facebook Janice simply might not be the same Janice on my Ancestry dashboard.

This did not stop me from doing as complete a written family tree as I could. Janice was my closest Jewish relative, and through mildly laborious searching, I found her mother's obituary, which mentioned her siblings' names, father's family names, and hometown nearby in Jersey. With this, I started an ongoing patchwork of scribble notes with minimal leads that surfaced over the next two years.

CHAPTER SEVENTEEN

PACIFIC BUDDY BOND

My other main lead was my mother's friend Trish. I had a quick weekend trip scheduled back to the west side of Oregon for a reunion with crew teammates from years past, and made plans to meet up with my mom in Portland afterward.

It had been five months or so since the original genetic results had come back, and we'd had multiple phone conversations but Deb and I both felt we needed to connect in person. A visit with Trish would be a perfect way to see each other, to provide Deb and Trish an opportunity to reconnect, and a potential opportunity to gather some new information for myself.

My best college buddy Conor, who had recently moved to the greater Portland area, picked me up from PDX and it took me no time to open up about my recent genetic discovery. Con and I had become like brothers through our twenties—even our families became strongly connected. We visited each other's homes multiple times through the years, and his little brother once stepped in as a last-minute winter formal dance date for my youngest sister, Lena, a short whim of a seven-hour trip from Seattle to Joseph, Oregon.

Con himself was the product of quite a story of circumstance. His parents met while waiting at a bus stop during a rare Seattle blizzard in the early eighties. His future mom and dad chatted and even exchanged names. Feeling like a connection was made, once they got back home they individually and hurriedly searched the Emerald City's phone book. Astonishingly, there they were, one immediately after the other in the thick white pages, during the days when white pages were still vitally useful, Eileen Bullinger and Ken Bullis.

A few years later, with a big smile and a contagious positive jubilation for life, Conor Bullinger Bullis (our ongoing joke, that's a lot of Bull) took his first breath. His mom dubbed him Conny Cakes, and I liked to remind him of the nickname with a loving tease. Zuzu Byrd Moro has the similar middle name maternal nod, like Conor.

Anyway, Conor got teary eyed as I opened up about the recent news of my DNA. I hadn't shared the news with many people outside my immediate family, the cousin group chat, and the Moros, who helped by providing their Ancestry results. Speaking of which, when my second Ancestry confirmation test came back after the Moros had shared theirs, my Uncle Jimmy did not populate as a relative, confirming again the lack of Moro genetics.

Cakes said, "D, wow man, I'm so blown away, are you okay? I mean wow," then he backpedaled a bit. "It doesn't change anything with your parents, I mean, your parents are your parents, but wow."

His heartfelt and honest reaction put me in a place that I often found myself over the next few years. I felt an almost obligatory need to reassure, to support those who cared about me, and my family, that we were all good. At the end of the day, I wouldn't be here, nor would I be the human I was, if things hadn't gone how they did. So, who was I to wish or think anything differently?

Con said he understood. He was one of the rare people who agreed with me on wanting to know the full story. Maybe our cohabitation experience in our college years had nurtured a tendency to view things like this as an adventure versus seeing it as something we may not want to uncover. As I said, this Bullinger Bullis was all positivity, whether it was his parents' real-life *Sleepless in Seattle*-esque story that shone through him, or just growing up where the sun was such a rarity one had to be their own beam of light. He could only see the positive, and it was as refreshing as being back in the rainy Pacific Northwest.

Shifting his pickup down the interstate north of Portland, kind smile on his face, Conor continued to reiterate how crazy the entire thing was, to go thirty-five years without knowing and then have all of this information fall in your lap.

It made me think, again, how this situation really was crazy—but it could be a good crazy. I was also hit by the level of surprise those closest to me had at the news. Con had always accepted and known only the truth that was presented, as had other close buddies. They never second-guessed my genetics. This knowledge helped me to not feel as blindsided by the news, or as if I were stranded on an island of naivety. Even if my aunts, uncles, and cousins seemed to be in the loop, my friends were in the same boat as I was—and maybe I wasn't as stupid as I felt for simply believing what was presented.

I explained that I was motivated to search not only for the adventure of seeking the truth, for Zu and also for this dude who never knew he might have a child out there. I wanted him to at least be presented with the information. He nodded. "But, D, what about your dad? How is he doing with all of this?"

"I think good, man, like, he had to know there was potential for this, right?"

"Ya, I guess so, but think about it, D, he changed his entire life to be your dad, and he's been an awesome dad for you."

Con could speak firsthand to this, based upon personal experiences from dads' weekends with my pops playing "butt darts" drinking games, late-night hot tubs, and freezing football games (perpetually playing second fiddle to the early-2000s USC dynasty).

Con and I had been through enough to have honesty and connection. He taught me the sport of crew, having been a rower on Lake Washington in high school, and was pivotal in my finding joy and self-confidence through being a member of a crew team. It was Con who moved into my dorm and chose to room with me. He lofted his bed, which was the pilot for his sophomore-year scheme to rent loft kits to freshmen (potentially just a tactic to meet new frosh ladies).

One night he was up on the top bunk when, at around two in the morning, I heard the rustling of the blinds from our third-floor window. Having finished his last final Conor had partied the night away, while I was trying to crunch some vital sleep before my last couple tests the next morning. He'd cracked the window, but a faded Con didn't realize he wasn't aiming out the window and, half dazed, sent a golden shower of semi-metabolized Killian's Irish Red raining down on me. A fitting pre-finals alarm clock.

His perspective on Johnny's place in this dynamic made me, once again, recalibrate my angle and discretion, but I couldn't pivot or pump fake. I felt the need to do everything I could to get to the rim and attempt to score some truth.

He understood, and let me know he was there for me if I needed anything. I probably wittily replied something like, ya, thanks dude, if you could just hook me up with Ruhi's last name I'll call that good, and he grinned back, "I got you, D."

TRISH'S TABLE

After the rowing reunion, my mom picked me up from Cow-town, Corvallis, and we headed north up the I-5 corridor to P-town, where it had all started for us. My mom is loving, gentle, kind, and a talker. For me she is the best road tripper out there, because she's a steady driver, she enjoys good tunes, and our conversation easily flows over state borders.

We talked the entire way about how we had both been feeling. Like so many times, I felt a sound connection that we were on the same page as we continued forward. She was willing to do anything to help in my search if I felt motivated to keep pursuing. She spoke of my pops, saying he loved me so much as well, and would always support me. She explained that if he had a slight aversion to all of this it was only because he wants me to be his and all his.

Off the exit near Trish's house, we rolled her way over skinny, winding roads slick with recent rain and lane lines covered in pine needles. Trish and her home were true *Portlandia* nostalgic treasures. She was hunched and slight of frame, with coarse grayed hair, a compassionate smile, and a kindhearted demeanor. Inside her home lived a plethora of plants, along with original murals and skylights everywhere. We settled into her warm, welcoming kitchen over some hot tea.

Trish's son leaned against the counter, a kind and quiet little dude who had never left home. He occasionally tried to help with names as Trish struggled to remember anything about Ruhi. She and Deb enjoyed reconnecting about their Premie group and days spent sewing. I thanked her again for her willingness to help, and asked if she had a chance to talk with any of the other Premies who had followed Guru Maharaj Ji along with my mom.

Trish said she had reached out, but no one had any recollection of a man named Ruhi. She and her son gave me a list of about five other group members who had attended in the eighties but faded away at varying points in life. I wrote the names down and quickly began Googling to see if I could find an active phone number for any of them.

Upon finding three contacts, two personal numbers, and one through his pottery website, I speaker dialed them as the four of us patiently awaited an answer. None of the softhearted people on the other end of the cell waves had any answers in our query about Ruhi. Providing light that if Trish herself had no knowledge of Ruhi, no other Premies would either.

As we parted ways, we thanked each other and shared well wishes. Trish promised future help, should anything arise.

I catalogued these new names in my phone and notes for the future as I flew out of the Pacific Northwest. However, I was nearly half a year into my search and my main two leads—Trish and Janice—seemed like a desert of dryness in stark contrast to my window-seat view of the perpetually rainy terrain below.

Before I boarded the plane, my mom had given me a good hug, I told her how much I loved her and appreciated everything she was doing for me now, and everything she'd done throughout my life. She smiled and conveyed the same feelings. She reiterated that we would always be there for each other, reminding me our love for each other is the most valuable thing in our lives.

CHAPTER EIGHTEEN

SEARCHING FOR THE NEEDLE

Having struck out on my closest Jewish genetic relative and the one person from my mother's past who may have known the traveling wanderer Ruhi, it was back to the drawing board.

My next step was to start reaching out to potential third cousins who had been identified through genetic testing. I started sending out mass messages similar to what I had sent to Janice.

I meticulously tracked each message sent and person awaiting responses. Although maybe not as meticulously as I perceived, because over the first year I received a couple of messages from people reiterating that they were sorry they could not help with any information but, as they had stated before, they had no knowledge of a relative named Ruhi.

At this point, I was doubling up and exhausting all options in the search, as bleak as they may seem. I had repurposed my late-night wind-downs into internet searches and reshuffling through the genetic connections showing up on 23andMe and Ancestry. At one point I had memorized the names of the top ten closest Jewish relatives on each site, as distant as fifth cousins, so upon logging on I could quickly ascertain if any new relatives had populated in the last twenty-four hours. I would cycle through the list, saying the names in my mind before my eyes examined the list, which almost never changed.

I held on to hope that, on any given night, I might find a new connection that would be the key to unlocking my search, now in stalemate. I'd spend the last hour of nearly every evening, and sometimes three or four hours, or random intervals of free time throughout the day, searching the only things I knew in different orders. "Ruhi Poet Portland Oregon 1982", or "Ruhi (with any family names that showed up in my genetic connections)", or "Poetry Portland Jewish", and what felt like thousands of other iterations of the same. I would type in literally any search I could come up with and, before long, the same searches cycling three, four, or five times.

As more time passed, I had memorized twenty-plus genetic relatives by full name and genetic cM's connection, and I had developed a mental image of the potential connection I craved—but the outlook was bleak and getting bleaker. I occasionally stumbled upon a random lead, like a professor at the University of Portland who had written something about Jewish people, or a lawyer in Portland who had the name Ruhi, or Ruhi was part of his Middle Eastern last name, or a female professor of poetry at University of Oregon in her mid-thirties who I could easily rule out.

Whenever I found a lead, I would devote multiple days, and sometimes weeks, trying to exhaust any research resources I could muster. Usually I'd end up with a random picture or a complete dead end. It would be a situation where the man had just moved to Portland in the last few years, or he was only in his forties. I found pictures of a couple of men who were long stretches based on what info I could find, but because of their age or location somewhat fitting the profile, I still had a prayer there was potential. I texted their pictures to my mom with a caption of, any chance this could be Ruhi? Both times there were quick responses from Deb, "No, that's not him."

Mom's dismissals were a bit tough for me. I had tempered expectations, of course, but it was hard to understand how, nearly forty years later, she could be so certain that someone was not him when her only recollections were that he was a poet who went by Ruhi and he looked like the Jesus paintings.

Plus, I wasn't so sure I trusted her memory. Not that I believed she was being intentionally inaccurate, but I knew a fuzziness exists in memory over many years. For her, this was evidenced by her immediate reaction that both the poet and Trish were already probably deceased. Now, of course, it's possible she was correct that he had passed, whether she knew so or just through simple math. He was older than her, and he seemed to have led a hard life without typical security (finances, shelter, etc.) that can ease aging. To Deb and Trish, the few people I knew of who knew him in his younger years, he seemed like a ghost.

COULD THERE BE OTHERS?

As the months went on, another seed of hope—or, at minimum, an interesting angle—began to grow. I was still waking up each day to check Ancestry and 23andMe with the possibility that a new relative, having taken their own saliva test months prior, could have populated. Furthermore, what if this person wasn't just another second or distant cousin, but someone genetically closer?

A light bulb had come on, shining on the reality that I could potentially have other half siblings out there. If I was the spawn of a seemingly fictional character going by the name Ruhi, perhaps someone else could be as well. Suddenly strangers might have the potential to be more than that. Of course, with nearly 8 billion people out there, the proverbial needle in the haystack seemed like the needle in the endless plains of the entire Dakotas wheat fields and beyond. But what if?

Now I'd added a fourth reason to pursue the unknown. Connecting with other, unknowing relatives who might be interested in forming pseudo-family relationships now joined my list of other reasons: Zu, now only months away from her June 2019 birth, adventure, and just treatment of Ruhi.

CHAPTER NINETEEN

INEVITABLE CONCESSION

As the days passed with a continued lack of close connections, I exhausted genetic distant cousins with similar messages.

I reached out to Phillip with three last names from Ukraine; Harvey L from Pennsylvania; Yifaht K from Toronto, Ontario; William F. from California; Gennidy G from Europe; Suzanne R from Uzbekistan; to name a few. I went deep into the thousand-plus Jewish relatives, knowing the further down I went in my list of matches, the lower my chances of discovering a viable lead might be.

I went even deeper, becoming semi-obsessed. I sent out hundreds of messages and got returned correspondence on a handful. Typically, replies were similarly polite, saying something to the effect of how interesting my story was, but they were sorry, they didn't know of any family members with the name Ruhi. Others would ask me if I knew his last name. Politely, I would reiterate that, unfortunately, I did not have his last name. Both of us would deduce, without written word, how much more reasonable this search would be, and how much higher the chance of success, if I, in fact, did have his surname.

I did have some closer relatives trickle in on my ancestry lists over the next year, but one after another they were all on my maternal side—a fact easily distinguished, as they were not Jewish. In fact, five of the genetic relatives who popped up were people I knew firsthand, and had strong in-person relationships with: another first cousin (one of the tall six-foot-four types), the daughter of this first cousin, a daughter of a second cousin, and a daughter of my mom's first cousin, who I had visited for graduations and family reunions. None of whom were Jewish.

As cool as it was to continue to be reaffirmed that this genetic system was, in fact, legit, it didn't get me any closer to wrapping up my search, which was now becoming a bit consuming and intoxicating. I thought, what's up? Only Brinks and Groebers (my Grandma Lena's maiden name) are into genetics now? The Jews are out? At least, the Jewish relatives closest to me seemed to be done learning about their DNA.

Had I tainted the genetic pool by taking a dip in the water, and now there was a conspiracy against me? Like, did they know about me and didn't want any part? Anyway, what were the chances that some wandering, pseudo-homeless dude procreated with not only my mother but with another woman as well? Probably pretty low. And even if he had, what are the chances that person—one in 8 billion—decides, hey, I'm down to spit in a cup and give some company my genetic information just for giggles?

Heck, there were a lot of conspiracy theories circulating about what one's DNA was actually being used for or stored for. It was a fairly new frontier, after all. I had experienced a bit of healthy skepticism early on, and similar worries might have been enough to scare people away rather than encouraging them to dive in. Based on the half-off holiday special offers from both 23andMe and Ancestry, you wonder whether their business was booming.

Nevertheless, it didn't stop me from downloading my entire genome and uploading it to enough third-party sites that I may not even be able to accurately differentiate them all at this point. There was Genome.com, a Jewish database of some sort, Family Finder, Gedmatch, etc. I even joined a couple of Jewish lineage detective sites, but once again—no dice.

BUT WAIT...

It was March 18, 2019, and I had just finished my school teaching day. As had become a daily ritual, I clicked on the Ancestry tab that had become burned into my screen on my cell and laptop from always being open. There, up top on my dashboard, was a new relative.

Sandwiched between two maternal first cousins, Beverly C. was 49 percent Jewish and we shared 842 cM's. Genetically, we were as close as my first cousins. And we were twice as close as Janice, the only other Jewish relative who was in the ballpark of being able to shed some light on my imagined immediate family.

I could feel my chest pounding, the cliché line people use. But I genuinely did feel a warm hope rush over, I can only assume pushed from my excited beating heart. Under Beverly's name, in parentheses, it stated, "managed by JeTaunne L." Of equal importance, it said the last log on was that day. I paged down and, sure enough, I had another close new relative in my third cousin block, with 170 cM's, JeTaunne L. I quickly fired off the following message—twice:

Hi Beverly and JeTaunne,

I have been hoping for months now to have a strong relative show up with a Jewish background. I had no knowledge of having any Jewish blood when I did the test, as my dad as I knew it then is Spanish/Italian/Mexican. I soon found out that my biological father was a man who went by "Ruhi" and lived in Portland Oregon in 1982. I have been unsuccessful in tracking down any information about him at this point without a last name or possibly even first name.

Anyway, I would appreciate connecting, and any information you may have. I have two first cousins who have done Ancestry on my mother's side and they show the same amount of shared DNA as you, which has me believing we may be first cousins?

Thanks for your time, and looking forward to vising more. My cell is 541 908 3039 and my email is dylan.moro@k12.sd.us.

Not awaiting a response, I explored their profiles. Along with nearly half Jewish DNA, Beverly was 17 percent Scottish; 15 percent Cameroon, Congo and Western Bantu Peoples; 5 percent Mali; 4 percent Senegal; 2 percent Ivory Coast and Ghana; 2 percent Nigeria; 2 percent Wales; 1 percent Indigenous Americas—North; and 1 percent Ireland.

JeTaunne was 15 percent Jewish; 2 percent Germanic European; 13 percent English and Northwestern Europe; 9 percent Scottish; 18 percent Norway; 11 percent Sweden; 11 percent Northern Italy; 9 percent Cameroon, Congo, and Western Bantu Peoples; 4 percent Mali; 3 percent Benin and Togo; 2 percent Nigeria; 2 percent France; and 1percent Ivory Coast and Ghana.

Interesting. So much more diversity coursing through their blood than mine. During my months of Google searching, I learned the rarer a name, the more successful specific searches would be. One other crucial piece of info was that Beverly was eighty years old and JeTaunne was my age, then thirty-six. I immediately found numerous phone numbers and addresses, mostly centering on Wisconsin.

Wisco was a few states east of my current home in South Dakota. It's the home state of my mother-in-law, and it lives deep within our hearts as avid Pack fans. We once made the pilgrimage to the frozen tundra with Keen's family to fulfill her dad Harvey's lifelong dream of taking in a game. Think of the *Rudy* scene, when his dad shows up at Notre Dame with watery eyes exclaiming, "This is the most beautiful sight these eyes have ever seen." That was pretty much it, verbatim, with a quick scene cut to me and Jose, shirtless in the men's room at halftime, painting a G and B from nip to nip as a couple of 350-plus pound cheese-fed onlookers told us, "Wow, you boys must be really comfortable with each other." We were. The snow fell, the crowd's energy warmed, and it was awesome.

Anyway, at this point I was done worrying about reactions. I'd been waiting half a year for any new piece of tangible information to follow up on. For me, it felt like eons, so I had no hesitation eagerly calling every number I could find. "No longer in service," no ringtone, "no longer in service" times three. Then a voice, quiet and somewhat seemingly speculative. "Hello?"

That's all I needed. I jumped right in with my spiel.

"Hi, my name's Dylan. This is random, but I saw you pop up on Ancestry...any chance...?"

JeTaunne was tender. She told me she had done the genetics test with her grandmother to attempt to track down any potential info for Beverly. Her aging grandma had been adopted in a closed adoption from New York, and had no information on who her biological parents were. Her adopted parents had passed, and there was no adoption paper trail.

Again, who in 1940 would have had the future perspective to foresee a day, eighty years later, when one's genetics could be mapped out with a sample of saliva? I admitted I didn't have any answers either, but thought, based on our relative closeness in terms of cM's and Beverly's age, that perhaps her grandmother might be my half aunt. It's possible she was Ruhi's half sibling.

"The only thing she knows is that she was in an orphanage in New York until the age of five or six, then she got adopted," JeTaunne explained. "The family that adopted her lived in Pittsburgh. The couple didn't have any children."

While I didn't have concrete assurance of this theory, I could start to paint a mental image. Filling in my ongoing sheet of family tree info and connections, I envisioned a scenario where Ruhi's Jewish father may have had a close relationship that produced Beverly with what must have been a woman of African and Scottish descent.

A key piece to this theory was JeTaunne's corroboration that it was indeed strange in the 1940s for an African-American couple to be able to adopt a child who, in her words, appeared to be white.

> "What's really odd is that she was adopted by a Black couple. Even though my grandmother is mixed, she's so fair-skinned she doesn't look biracial at all. For a Black couple to adopt a Caucasian child in those days was unheard of. I always wondered if the family traveled to New York intentionally to adopt her because somehow she was related."

This, obviously, was not the final piece to the puzzle that I longed to discover. But it was a major enough connection, and it provided more hope and clarity to my potential family tree. I asked JeTaunne if Janice showed up on her connections. She said that Janice did and was, of course, a closer relative to Beverly than she was to me.

We exchanged gratitude and decided to stay in touch as we both attempted to find more information.

DEAL DAY: DEAL HOPE

Being overzealous, I immediately asked Keen, "Do you think I should try and go see them in person and connect at some point?"

As my sounding board of reasonability, she said something to the effect of, whatever you want, Dyl, but maybe just relax a bit and let it play out.

She was right—she always is, really. Spouses often say that, but she is. Relaxing was hard for me. I felt like I finally found something, but it was an off-ramp that just took me to another open-ended tunnel with no clear lighting and no tangible answers.

Perhaps, though, this was the start. I mean, they popped up today, who knows who might pop up tomorrow or next week or the following?

Well, in reality, it was the start of a massive dry spell, another desert oasis. Days, months, over a year, and no new connection of any more genetic closeness would materialize.

I didn't realize it then, but the newfound hopefulness that was flowing would slowly and kind of painfully dwindle day by day, month by month until the likelihood of finding Ruhi seemed lower and lower.

Amazon Prime Day deals with half-off 23andMe and Christmas 2019 with deals on Ancestry reinvigorated my hope that if the price was right maybe someone would be more intrigued to take the genetic leap, or to give the gift to another. I would be on the other side every night searching, every morning checking to see if anyone new popped up—nada.

CHAPTER TWENTY

RUHI'S POTENTIAL POEMS

I had uncovered one other possible lead with one of my original Google searches: "Ruhi Poem".

It's funny how changing one word, in this case poetry to poem, can produce such varying search results. The first might provide eighty-plus pages from an early-nineties Middle Eastern magazine in PDF form, with one little "Ruhi" on page 62. (A short, related search tangent, between 'Ruhi Portland and Jewish' searches, pages and pages of separate Portland- and University of Oregon-based Jewish magazines from decades past were quite a time suck to wade through, looking for a speck of gold and not truly knowing what this "gold" might even appear as.)

Whereas the search term "Ruhi Poem" produced an interesting lead right up top from a website called Hello: Poetry:

ruhi Apr 2016
dawn
early grays choke me uncertain
numb daybreak, phantom sheets
dipping into the cool crevices
your body used to fill

your breath once tasted sweet on my lips
but in morning fog it bleeds ice

dancing transient across my tongue
it breaks against this raw, hollow mouth

I curl into the shirt I never gave to you
frosted with empty memories —
stolen nights
sanguine skin
swirls of smoke escaping your fingertips
and your voice in my dream last night

someday it won't hurt but
this morning it is chilly sharp
hit me hard. nothing feels real anymore

Nine other poems followed, with references the ocean, saltwater kisses, and settling on a feeling of longing and loss. Much poetry tackles those themes, but as a reader with wavering hope I was fixated. Could this be the Ruhi? My Ruhi?

I immediately created an account to be able to message the person who posted the poems. I tried to look past the 2016 date in hopes the poster was still somewhat active three years later. I shared the poems with my mom, and called her immediately. She said, "It's interesting it makes you think it could be his writing, but I don't know."

She still had been unable to uncover the one physical relic from her past relationship with Ruhi, the book of poems he had gifted her titled *Petals of Light*. She held onto hope and assured me the book might be the answer to our questions. I grounded myself in an unconvinced reality. How could some book of random poems written forty years ago help at all with the search I was conducting through the conduits of technology and the internet?

Oh well. Blind faith—don't knock it, respect it, correct?

Anyway, I attempted to find some hidden meaning buried in the words of each of the poems. In my naivety, I might have thought that was the exact purpose of poetry. Maybe Ruhi was still longing for an answer to a lifelong hole that had been left within him. It's not too much of a stretch to think the man who came looking for my mother, having been told to move on, perhaps might still be writing poetry. Conceivably he could have morphed into the modern world and put his verses on the internet for someone searching to find. Seemed pretty far-fetched—and blatantly egocentric. But it was all I had at the time.

I gave it a few weeks, and no response, per usual. I attempted a different method. I would dust off my poetry pen, essentially dormant since middle school with the exception of a few years of songwriting in the mid-2000s, and I would post some poems about this search, this journey I was on. Surely the poetry world must be small enough that someone would know someone, I thought facetiously.

At this point, my mind was going to great lengths, as far as wondering if Ruhi himself might happen to Google his name, like many of us do from time to time, where he would come upon my messages and poetry and be led to connect.

They still remain online:

Dylan

Searching for ruhi Portland OR 1982

1 follower / 49 words

Follow Message Block

Stream

3

Poems

3

Favorites

2

Dylan Oct 5
Ruhi
Help me find my biological father
"Ruhi" Portland Oregon 1982

Dylan Jan 2019
Misplaced confusion
New year, parenting parents.
Find calm, find focus.
Distract complacency, motivate soul.
Forgiveness, patience.
Ruhi? Jewish?
Most have heavier burdens.
New year, new parent.

Dylan Nov 2018
Searching ruhi
Simple with control
Trust in pose but lost
Surrounding sensible
Driftwood unfamiliar

Where are you
Tangible methods perhaps
Lost on memories airbrushed
Ruhi, fiction, ruhi... fact?
— The End —

I even received a follower, Jen, shortly after posting. She shared some positive words about my writing. To be honest, these were written in a matter of minutes while doing my morning business, getting set to start the day. But art can flow from unrealized and inglorious places, regardless of time and effort allotted, right?

Am I one of the only people who think some poetry and, really, art in general seems like it could be fabricated in no time at all? It's almost like minimal efforts posing as art. Then again, art is in the eye of the…

At this point, I knew this was a stretch. The reality of how vast this search was, of the pointlessness of attempting to explore without hard facts, had settled in. My experiences with Janice, Trish, and Beverly were enough to see I was up against major hurdles and, in those cases, I had something tangible to go from. My current state—random internet searches and random poems by random people using the name Ruhi—was a pipe dream.

Heck, some of my strongest potential leads had been women named Ruhi in their twenties, a stark contrast to this older Jewish man who may have wandered into the forest one day in his forties or fifties and never returned. In fact, that scenario seemed as likely, or more likely, than me somehow finding him forty years later with some random searches on a screen.

POETRY ROOTS

Poetry is a gift in my family. My grandmother Lena wrote simple verses to capture feelings of gratification for new grandchildren and landing her first fish of the season on the shores of Steamboat Lake with Hahns Peak's reflection glistening. Recently my mom put together Grandma Lena's Poetry, including this verse:

Time – on my Mind

Time is of value,
When wise it is used
When time is wasted
It's value you lose.

Time is a gift,
One thankful should be
In using it wisely

Despite that it's free

Time is a healer
When passing so quick
We wish it away
Like one doing a trick!

Time is a pleasure
When doing the things,
We like better than others
And joy to us brings.

Time is a friend
Who's kindness goes deep,
Some not so kindly
Are harder to keep

Time is from God,
To seek and to pray
For living our lives,
HIS will to obey!

Lmb '82

My sister Lena inherited the gift along with Grandma's name, and my pops
recently said how great this poem remains:

It rests inside my room all day
Constantly quiet, longing to be played
Its golden strings shine in the light
The long smooth neck, curved body so bright
A wooden yellow it reflects
Scrapes, knocks, unintended dents
It's hollow soul a weeping friend

With a small round hole like a mouth that vents

The tuning keys, frets and a bridge

A mechanical magic that yearns to live

When it's lonely it calls my name

And when I am, I do the same

It waits for my hands to work with ease

A special art, a familiar technique

The music is bliss with every strum

An imaginative melody and constant hum

Our spirits they fit was we share our passions

One a purpose, one a fashion

But so much more, will it ever know

That I use it as a tool for individual growth

And even more it is my best friend

Who knows all my secrets, never judges or pretends

Every emotion and every feel

A relationship like a circle or wheel

That spins around so easily

As we both perform so carefully

Fulfilling each of our desires

My prized possession I do admire

Debra's alter egos, Doodles Doodly Dootsker and Ribbons the Clown, took fun-loving rhymes and made them instant singalongs for her daycare kids and extended family. Our four-generational family sing along anthem was a Debra original:

Never Had a Blanket

Never had a blanket keep me warm as you do
Never had a fire warm my insides
Never had a warm wind

To blow me o'er the mountain
To sail the ocean on the other side…

Sleepin' with you in the evening
It's hard to close my eyes
But wakin' to you in the morning time
I'd say it's harder to leave your side…

'Cuz I never had a blanket keep me warm as you do
I've never had a firm warm my insides
Never had a warm wind
To blow me o'er the mountain
To sail the ocean on the other side…

There's a few things that I like and most-of-all
It's kissin' and whisperin' and listenin'
Tonight we'll dance underneath the moonlight
Across the water on the mountain's other side

'Cuz I've never had a blanket keep me warm as you do
I've never had a fire warm my insides
You are the warm wind
That blows me o'er the mountain
To sail the ocean on the other side
Yes, you are the warm wind
That blows me o'er the mountain
To sail the ocean on… the other side…

It was commonplace to tuck a short verse into a Christmas poem, or turn notable numbers into catchy rhymes, such as Dylan and Keena June Nineteena's wedding date. We were not wordsmiths, but a rhyme left a smile and helped imprint a memory. My G-pa Brink had a few good ones.

"Kindness is to do and say, the kindest thing in the kindest way.
Be a good boy, live a good life. Be a good husband, find a good wife.
Be a good girl, live a good life. Marry a good husband, be a good wife."

In middle school, living in my mom's hometown of Plankinton, South Dakota, I sent off a few rhymes that were published in the statewide middle school poetry book. One poem titled "Why?" was simply question after question about commonsense observations. The other was called "Poor Boy," a look at a young boy growing up in the grips of poverty.

During the circle game, all of us used words with slight rhyming to construct original tunes that became family anthems. The ease of finding a rhyme seemed intrinsic. It was also a skill that was modeled and nurtured, but seemed to flow naturally. At the time I didn't think much about the importance of words to my family and bloodline.

HOARDING DELUSION

My mom has always been a bit of a hoarder. To be fair, I would dub her a somewhat clean and organized hoarder, and also a self-improving hoarder, as her piles were becoming fewer and fewer.

For this reason, it seemed logical to me that maybe she could find this book of poems. I was highly skeptical anything would come out of the book to link to the present day. But, at minimum, it would be a physical trinket that I could not only hold, but read. I could study his penmanship and work, and possibly compare it to other writings for similarities.

Furthermore, what if he had planted within his writing some future message for a meeting or a reunion of sorts? Could I break the code of his poetry to produce our reunion? This idea seemed as delusional as it was hopeful. Again, months had passed, then a year, and mom still had yet to uncover this book of poems.

My mom was the woman who could find any picture of any day in our family history, or the flannel my pops was wearing in October of 1981 in the Water Tower District of Portland. Yet, she couldn't find this book of poems by Ruhi.

I started doing some mental gymnastics of compare and contrast. If this book could not be found in her humble three-bedroom, one bath, which held maybe a maximum of twenty different boxes, a dozen or so bags, and three suitcases, then how was I going to find a human—especially when the jury was still out on him being alive—somewhere in this entire planet of billions of other humans? If it were a bet, I would take finding the book over finding the dude.

All that being said, I wasn't going to stop. My daughter had yet to formally ask a question, but I could see the day when that might come to be, and that was all the motivation I needed to push on.

Push push, rage rage into the night, against the dying of the light--another Dylan. In fact, later someone posed to me that the poet Dylan Thomas was the reason the Zimmerman dude took the Dylan name. And that, in turn, would be the reason I was a Dylan. Or a Dyl-bob-squared, or a Dylmoflo, or a St. Dylano, or a Dyl-pickle, or a Big D with Sports (my middle school penname writing the sports shorts for the local Plank paper).

CHAPTER TWENTY-ONE

THE LIGHT SIDE OF THE DISTANT COUSIN CONNECTION FORCE

My leads seemed to have run dry. I did have some ongoing conversations with distant cousins, some of whom sincerely wanted to help but didn't have any tangible information to make a difference. Still, the kind gestures and support of people I had never met, but with whom I shared a distant genetic connection, helped continue to fuel my search.

Others periodically checked in and provided perspective that my search wasn't completely pointless. As days and months passed with no new connections, these check-ins helped me keep a sliver of hope.

I could see similarities between my search for genetic answers and a detective trying to solve a crime. The discovery of fresh evidence brought the highest potential for cracking the case, but as time faded away, the likelihood of solving seemed to diminish.

One distant cousin I corresponded with, Suzanne from Uzbekistan, was interesting. I was able to be an onlooker as she traveled her own genetic journey to track down more information on her sperm-donor father.

Here is our correspondence over a few years

July 27, 2019

SUZANNE: Thank you so much for connecting, Dylan!

I wonder if, by elimination, you can tell me if the Ashkenazi Jewish background would have been through your mother or your father. Any idea?

Mine is through my biological father, who would have been an athletic medical student (probably in Philly) in the late '50s/early '60s.

I'm curious, Dylan, about "Ruhi." I don't know Hebrew, but it's closely related to Arabic and though mine is rusty, my Kazakh is quite 'fresh' and that name means, "my spirit." It's an endearing term used with someone really close, as in 'darling' or 'sweetheart.'

July 28, 2019

DYLAN: That's really interesting info, Suzanne, thanks for sharing. My biological father would be the side with the Ashkenazi Jewish lineage. From what I know of him he's probably in his seventies and was in Portland, Oregon, in 1982 and went by the name Ruhi.

Reading your bio, your story is also very interesting, Suzanne. I wish you the best with your search for more information. It's definitely an interesting trip when you get scientific data back that is different from what you have grown to know as factual, but I suppose a bit exciting as well. Are you on Ancestry? I've found some closer family connections by doing that as well.

Take care.

SUZANNE: Yes! You get it, Dylan! Such a mishmash of emotions. The carpet has been pulled up from under me, yet I'm finding the weave in that carpet is so much more complicated (and interesting) than I ever imagined.

Yes. Some of my half siblings (maternal and paternal) are on Ancestry.com. I have ordered a kit but because I live outside of the U.S., it is being brought to me. I think by September I should be able to connect via that network.

Would love to hear more about how you have discovered your own surprises.

Are your parents who raised you alive and able to answer questions?

Hmm, OK, based on the data and comparing with my paternal/maternal half siblings, I think it's safe to say that our fathers were possibly second cousins. My paternal half-siblings and I are in our late fifties now. (In 1983 I was a freshman in college.) My biological father was probably at the peak of his medical career (if he graduated) about the time that your father was in Portland, Oregon.

By the way, has your mother intimated that you might have been a sperm donor baby, like my siblings and I? I'm just curious how you've gotten the information you have. When I found out, I questioned whether the siblings telling me of our 'unique' birth were intimating that mom had been unfaithful to our dad, but all four of the kids in the family in which I was raised were sperm donor babies. One brother has refused genetic testing but an examination of the DNA of his son/my half nephew and that of my other brothers leads us to assume that we have four different Ashkenazi Jewish fathers. Philadelphia medical schools had a high percentage of Jewish students back in the day.

July 29, 2019

DYLAN: I think you're right about the second cousin level of relation for our fathers, pretty cool. My parents are both still around, in fact, they visited just last week as we had our first child. My mom had two partners, one being my biological father and one being the man who raised me as my dad. When I was born they just believed that I was his and raised me as such and until I got the test didn't speculate too hard that it could have been the man who went by Ruhi.

My mom describes him as kind of a traveling-through, kind man who she really knew nothing about terms of name, profession, or anything like that but was very caring. They were part of a spiritual group that would meet weekly that had nicknames. My parents are both very open and honest so it's been okay talking about it. For my dad that's raised me I think it's been harder. He says he wishes he hadn't known, but I think deep down they must have had questions throughout, as I look like my other three siblings (all from them) but there are differences for sure.

So far, the closest I've gotten to clarification is a lady in Wisconsin named Beverly who shows up on Ancestry as closely related as a first cousin, I believe her to be my half aunt and my biological father's half-sister. She was part of a closed adoption, so she knows no information on family names other than that it happened in New York.

I do have another relative that has about half the genetic relatedness of Beverly, who lives in Massachusetts, that I tried to reach out to but either doesn't know or doesn't want to share information. I think she could actually be the key until somebody else populates. So, I kind of just wait patiently to see if maybe somebody will show up. That's the exciting and interesting part, I guess, that I could have half-siblings out there. Just having our first daughter, I definitely would like to have some information to be able to tell her, but we'll just try to be honest about what I know at the point she can start to understand.

Thanks for sharing your experience. It's definitely cool to hear other people that are open and interested enough to pursue their lineage. At the end of the day, I just feel thankful that I'm here one way or another and that I had people who were willing to care for and love me.

Also, the Jewish connection has been really interesting for me, as I really have no firsthand experience with Jewish people or the religion. But it's such a unique fascinating lineage and there is so much connection between relatives. I think it's kind of cool for all your siblings to have that in common—also interesting that those medical Philly Jewish men were willing to donate. Has any one of your siblings shown close relations through the donation to other people they were unaware of? Could you be similar to me, and potentially have other half siblings? I've heard stories of donor sperm connecting siblings later in life.

Also, there are some resources for people of Jewish descent to connect that I've tried but had minimal new information. You essentially upload your DNA data from 23andMe or Ancestry and then they have a pool to connect with, but it doesn't seem any more in-depth than what already populates. There's also a DNA detectives' group on Facebook that somebody suggested I reach out to that I tried. They said that I didn't have a case that they would take on, but may be worth looking into for you if interested. Take care, if I can do anything to help down the road keep in touch.

September 1, 2019

SUZANNE: Hey, Dylan! Sorry to have been out of the loop for a while.

I just wanted to point out that my half siblings showed up as 'first cousins.' It makes sense. Instead of four shared grandparents, as typical whole siblings would, we have just two grandparents in common. I wonder if Beverly might just be a half-sister of yours ... just saying.

So, the relative in Massachusetts, is that person on 23&Me? What name was given? I'm wondering if they might be included in my relative lists.

September 6, 2019

DYLAN: Suzanne, thanks for getting back and way cool about your half siblings. I looked into that as well for Beverly, but she's eighty years old and I'm thirty-six, hence why I'm thinking half aunt (possibly half sibling to my biological father). The relative in Mass is Janice Wertheimer, but she is on Ancestry not 23andme. Other than that, still waiting to see if someone populates eventually. Anyway, thanks for corresponding and take care.

Janice Wertheimer
1st–2nd Cousin

Shared DNA: 440 cM across 23 segments

Beverly Cargile
Managed by JeTaunne Lott
1st–2nd Cousin

Shared DNA: 843 cM across 39 segments

September 7, 2019

SUZANNE: Good point about Beverly's age—but that makes Janice even further away, genetically.

I just was notified that my Ancestry sample has been received. Looks like another six to eight weeks for results. Looking at shared DNA, I place Janice as Ruhi's potential half cousin, I think. — Suzanne

November 21, 2019

DYLAN: Hey Suzanne, I just had a note from you that I must have missed before, how's it been going? I think you are correct about Janice and Ruhi, what is your connection with Janice in terms of genetics? Hope things are going good, my cell is 541 908 3039, if you ever would rather communicate using text or call. Anyway, take care

January 27, 2020

SUZANNE: Dear Dylan,

Wow! Can't believe I haven't followed through! Please forgive my lapse. Lots has happened since I last wrote in September! We found my bio dad and have had contact via e-mail. My two (half) sisters and I who found each other via 23&Me wrote a 'joint' letter and got a very kindhearted response from our dad, who wishes to retain (as much) anonymity (as possible) in order to protect family members on whom this could potentially have a negative effect.

So, questions just seem to birth more questions—but, apparently, he has had seven children. Five of us via sperm donorship.

Three of us are in contact, as I mentioned. The two brothers via sperm donorship are not. As far as I know, his two children via marriage do not know we exist (and one of them is married to a celebrity and so it's probably best to drop it anyway. I don't like the idea of this hitting the media). My own mother is not too keen on things that were supposed to be hidden becoming public fare.

We've found some really friendly cousins who have helped us tremendously, provided pictures and given some background information. I think there are some things of which even our bio dad has never been informed. Really makes me feel like a 'voyeur' in some ways. I'm struggling to find that line between idle curiosity and reasonably tracing roots.

Any news on your end? How is life as a 'new' father? May you treasure every moment!

Dylan: Hey Suzanne, sounds like a lot of awesome info you've discovered. I'm happy for you. Nothing new on my end, I've had some people pop up, but all on my mother's side. It's way cool all of the extended family you are finding. Zuzu is seven months now and we are loving every moment, even the 3 a.m. screaming, ha. Take care and keep in touch.

I was happy for Suzanne. She had uncovered an interesting story that wrestled with some similar dynamics of unknown information between genetically related family members. My story was yet to unfold, and it fundamentally differed in terms of the nature of the relationships between our mothers and our biological fathers. I was genuinely happy for her to have uncovered truths and to have formed connections with others sharing the experience.

THE DARK SIDE OF THE DISTANT CONNECTION FORCE

Some of the correspondence, though, was less optimistic. I attempted to reach out to any genetic relatives, no matter the distance, and with thousands of distant Jewish "cousins" between the Ancestry and 23andMe platforms, I looked for any shade of potential.

One dude, frlogan58, was a way distant cousin with only 11 cM's over two chromosome segments total. In other words, we may have had a shared grandparent five to eight generations back, but I dug deep through his profile the way I do for all relatives and found the name Ruhi on one of his family trees. Logically, I thought it might be worth a shot.

At this point, I was hoisting prayer three-pointers from anywhere on the court—desperate times, desperate measures. If nothing else, I wanted to feel confident that I had depleted all potential options. I kept pressing on, no matter how small the chances were. I had no choice. Again, with no surname I had no real potential for directed internet searches, and no close relatives had populated in two years besides Beverly and her closed adoption.

Anyway, frlogan58 shared the following, which was a fairly common response for a dead end—though his had a much darker turn:

September 13, 2019

> **DYLAN:** Hello, I've been attempting to track down my biological father. He was in Portland, Oregon, in 1982 and went by Ruhi, I do not have a surname. Thanks for any help.

September 27, 2019

> **FRLOGAN58:** My Ruhi was born in 1972, never lived in Portland.
> OCTOBER 1, 2019
>
> **DELILAHLOGAN:** Hi Dylan, I'm writing for my son. Your matches with Ruhi are from the European-Jewish side of the family. We have not identified how the Jewish ethnicity entered the family, but suspect Ruhi's great grandfather was the Jewish

overseer of a plantation where he impregnated the Black great-grandmother. There is no documentation for this theory, of course. We can tell the Jewish ethnicity is linked to the Black side of the family from the DNA matches.

You being a remote cousin really disqualified our Ruhi as being as close family as a father.

I wish you luck in your search for your father. My Ruhi was named for a friend from Iran. So, it is not a Jewish name. If you are not getting close matches that are helpful, check out Gedmatch.com, a free website that gives matches from all of the DNA testing sites.

OCTOBER 2, 2019

DYLAN: Thanks for getting back to me and your insights. I tried Gedmatch in past, but had no luck. Thanks, and take care.

I tried not to let dead ends, especially strange ones, bum me out too bad. After all, if nothing else, I was resilient. It did make my mind wander. Was I playing with fire? What if what I found was ultimately more negative than positive? I felt confident that I could handle it. Thanks to my family support system, I was already so grounded that it was bound to be manageable. That being said, in dark moments I could slip into the thoughts of "what if." What if my bloodline is somehow populated by terrible criminals with psych problems? Could my blood share DNA with a killer, or worse?

As I considered these potential twists, I thought about other humans who were burdened by the negative historical actions of their forefathers. Would something like that really change who I was? Or would it just add a darker layer that I then would feel obligated to dismiss, rectify, or cover up? This was not in my nature—or, should I say, my "nurture"—I valued transparency. But, then again, was there a reason Janice W. hadn't been pumped to connect?

Transparency, to me, is one of the most valuable characteristics in gaining trust, and it would have the most important purpose to me in the journey I had embarked on over the past two years.

I suppose transparency and honesty were deep within me, nurtured from a young age as my parents took us to places like Rainbow Farm, a hippie commune in the woods between the coast and Eugene, Oregon. Here, multiple families raised their kids living in huts, repurposed school buses, and glorified tents. They'd grow food and create crafts to sell at the weekly Saturday market in Eugene. We would go to hang out with the kids of the midwife who helped in the home-births deliveries of my three younger siblings.

We were set free to make bows and arrows, hike through the woods, and just explore our surroundings. The same group of people helped hook my parents up with running the daycare booth at the Oregon Country Fair, a summertime hippy fest in the woods outside Eugene. There, I jumped into hacky-sack circles with welcoming fairgoers while topless fire dancers twirled their lit sticks nearby.

There was a level of trust with everyone around at these events that was imprinted on us kids. We knew we were in a safe place with others of like mind and acceptance. It was a freedom with transparency and trust, but just like in any situation, our naivety could have been preyed upon.

Fortunately, my memories are happy and positive, but a generation later while raising my toddler daughter, it seems commonplace to analyze my parents' choices. I tend to mirror the positive while setting mental barricades to change choices deemed as unnecessary risks. I imagine my parents once did the same. Zu will surely judge some silly things her mother and I are currently doing, even if we're exercising self-perceived parental best intentions.

Also, could I really be at core a transparent person, if my entire life, my origin story, was not built on transparency? I had always been told the truth about my birth from a given point of view, and, I was thirty-five before

I found another layer of the onion I hadn't been aware of. Now that layer seemed to have no end, so how transparent could I really be?

I suppose this phase of experiencing a sort of mental depression or confusion is normal when setting out on any pursuit. I told myself the most successful journeys include overcoming and learning from adversity. What doesn't kill, strengthens.

The only thing that was dying, more and more, was realistic hope. My motivation was there, but I was starting to feel hopeless about the idea that I had any control over this situational search. It was more than a needle in the haystack, or the plains of the Dakotas. I was looking for literally one of nearly 8 billion humans, who may have already passed with no digital or paper trail.

A wandering poet with no tangible connections or legitimate known name.

CHAPTER TWENTY-TWO

EXHAUSTION

With forty-plus search windows open on my phone and computer, I continued to drain all digital searches I could muster. I started new queries nearly every day, and picked up past searches that had reached dead ends or that never really had an end because they lacked a clear start.

I kept thinking, maybe if I pick the search up later something new might click. I hoped it might be like looking at a piece of art and then, suddenly, from a different angle or under new light, there is an entire new perspective. Or, like in coaching hoops, when we might run the same play hundreds of times before it clicked, or a shooter might throw a desperation full-courter when we're down by two at the buzzer and, that one time, it goes in for the win. So, I rationalized, why close the game? At least take the shot.

In a certain sense, as I retraced every search I could think of, I was in a controllable state of madness. It felt controllable in that I could compartmentalize everything until the house was quiet and my daily work had wound down and obligations were taken care of, but the search was a nightly ritual from 8:30 to 10...or later. Then I'd pick back up again in the morning when getting ready to start the day with "toilet time" (a gross habit, but it was a good chance to see if any new relatives had populated in the previous twenty-four hours). It felt like unwrapping a gift that was another empty box day in, day out.

I tried to use the name searches my mom had thought she could see in her inner mind: "Lawrence, Martin, Ruhi." I'd been through what felt like hundreds of pages of the comedian Martin Lawrence. "Poet 1982 Portland

Oregon Ruhi"—nada. "New York Ruhi W[Janice's last name]—nope. I started to plug Ruhi in front of the last name of every relative who was shared on Ancestry and 23andMe—a tedious process, but I just thought, what if?

A couple times, 23andMe and Ancestry did updates on their genetic platforms, further breaking down DNA or showing maps of where relatives were located. My DNA breakdown didn't change and no new pathways opened, but the map was interesting and seemed like it could potentially help. I exhausted messages to all relatives from the Pacific Northwest, no matter how distant their cM's. Washington, Oregon, even Cali. Then I proceeded to the New England states, and there were a lot of them, and even Nebraska, on a whim because my mom had mentioned maybe he had traveled to or from there, but again nothing.

RANDOMNESS REPRODUCED?

One interesting marker stuck out when the map function was created. A person I knew popped up from my wife's little hometown, Kadoka, South Dakota, which we had called home for eight years until just the past year. Karen, my mother-in-law, worked in the school district with this distant cousin's wife. In fact, I even taught science to his stepdaughter and coached her in hoops. At first, I dismissed the person as it was a distant cousin (a fourth to sixth cousin with shared DNA 22 cM across three segments). I also reasoned they must be on my mother's side, since her family originated from So-Dak and her family tree had many branches.

But upon further investigation, there was a most interesting caveat to this connection. Our correspondence is below.

January 8
2:38 PM

> **DYLAN:** Karen showed me that you show up as my relative—
> that's crazy and cool. I assumed it would be on my mom's side,

since she is from Plankinton and has many cousins in SD—but even more strange, it is on my biological father's side, who I believe is fully Jewish. I had no idea about being half Jewish until I did the genetic test. My dad who raised me is Italian/Spanish. Do you have any knowledge of connection on the side of your family? Anyway, hope things are good and take care.

Side note, I saw Lanie play against Philip last night on the livestream, she played really well

January 10
1:49 PM

COUSIN: That is crazy. When we first got the results, we saw John Moro from Spearfish and didn't think anything of it. My wife said, maybe he's related to Dylan. Ha ha, who knew? We don't know anything about my birth father, that's why I did this test. The closest relative it shows is a second cousin, so we haven't learned anything yet. The adoption agency did tell my parents I was Jewish, and that they thought the guy was a son to a rabbi. That's all we know.

January 15

DYLAN: Interesting and, ya, what a small world. Meant to come chat with you guys at the ballgame, I'll try and catch you next time. I hope you find some more info eventually. It's kind of exciting thinking other relatives might pop at some point. Take care.

This exchange renewed my sense of hope and motivation. After all, this guy had taken one of the genetic tests I had taken as well; casting my net wide with the two most popular companies was starting to pay off a bit.

And if a random person from a town of 650 people, someone I personally knew, was not only Jewish—which is crazy rare in the Midwest small town world—but also, in the epitome of random chance, was actually a relative of mine, maybe just maybe I could find my needle in the haystack.

Heck, most nights on *SportsCenter Top Ten* some high school kid from Tennessee or Utah is throwing in a full-court miracle of a buzzer-beater winner.

It could happen.

THE CREW CONNECTION

The best part of my first undergrad experience at Oregon State University was getting to be a member of the crew team.

I was so late a bloomer, as I was exploring my early college days at the Oregon State freshman BBQ in 2001, a couple of six-foot-eight dudes asked me to talk to their coach solely based on my anti-intimidating stature. Coach had a simple Q for me: "Are you a mother-f'r?"

I said, "Come again?"

With a sly smile, Coach Kjell repeated, "Are you a mother f'r?"

I replied simply, "I suppose I can fit that roll."

Thus, I became a walk-on to the OSU men's crew team as a coxswain. My only former experience with crew was seeing the sixty-foot boats glide through the summer Olympics. As an eighty-seven-pound high school grad, I was being given the keys to be the "coach on the water" of a crew shell holding eight giant dudes. By springtime, for my initial weigh-in on the shores of San Diego's Mission Bay, I had beefed up to ninety-five pounds in time for our first regatta of the season.

By the time I was a senior at OSU, commanding the varsity eight, I had put on enough pounds I actually had to diet. I was pushing a healthy buck-forty and nudging above the six-foot mark, the tallest coxswain in the nation and taller than multiple rowers on our team. For a quick sec

I considered flipping the script and trying to become a rower, much like a coxswain I later coached at Williams College, but knew I didn't have the strength-to-size ratio to make a legit impact. My team supported me enough to be willing to carry the fifteen pounds of dead weight over the minimal 125 standard.

So I went from carrying twenty-five pounds of sand as a frosh to sweating it out in a honey bucket pre-race run to attempt to shed an extra pound of water. Every ounce counted over the six-minute, 2,000-meter course and might make the difference in a seat length. My humble brag today is that I have doubled my weight since graduating high school— from an eighty-seven-pound grad to 175 as of today. As a teacher for ten years, I have yet to see a middle- or high-schooler who was as small as myself during their teen years.

Because of rowing, now I was flying for the first time with best buddies to San Diego, to Wisconsin, and to New Jersey, where we lined up for a six-minute race against Olympic rowers from Ivy League schools.

It was the cliché experience of a lifetime. We were mostly homegrown Oregon dudes with no prior experience with rowing except what we might have caught during the Olympics. A few of us, like my buddy Con, were high school club rowers who found a great home at OSU because they were a little undersized to get recruited to the major programs across the country. Our men's team had no scholarship money. Dudes were on the team because they wanted to be and had made a committed choice, as there was no campus glory—if anything, the opposite. It was pure, it was hard work, and it was life changing in a most positive way.

As the "latest bloomer," my inept physical growth was what gave me the opportunity to steer the crew shell as the coxswain—if I'd weighed more than 125 pounds I would have been considered dead weight. Our coaches were the role models that most parents hope their college kids get to have. Their positive impact on our lives was immeasurable and everlasting. Coach Kjell played Miles Davis blues albums on road trips to races, took us to the best breakfast spots in Cali, and dropped us off at Ground Zero in NYC in the spring of 2002 to feel the gravity of the area and moment. Giving us buddy-system responsibility and a rendezvous point in the evening, he allowed us ten-plus hours to explore as much of the city as our legs could take us.

Later, Coach Fred had us over for his famous Jamaican jerk ribs. He also played on our intramural hoops team as our best defensive enforcer. A former Olympic boat captain, his competitive spirit was contagious. Both coaches went the extra mile and let visiting family members ride with them in their "launch," allowing them to watch our entire practice. It wasn't surprising, with all this support outside of the actual boat, that we were able to accomplish some great things inside the boat as well. We finished top ten in the nation each year from 2001 to 2005.

Because of its traditional act of jersey swapping, men's crew was one of the only sports not sanctioned by the NCAA. It was an act of pride and respect for each shell, upon crossing the finish line with rowers lurching over, gasping for breath, to pull over to the winning shell and gift the jerseys off our own backs. Each losing rower and coxswain gives their jersey to the winning counterpart who shared the same seat number. It was humbling. It also was beautiful. During my years, I accumulated quite the collection of mostly cotton jerseys from some very prestigious schools we had beaten.

One race stood out then and, in the "K-Bacon six degrees of separation," would come to impact my life sixteen years later as well.

CORNELL KARMA

In the spring of 2004, we headed to Rutgers for a time-trial competition called a head race, with a third crew being Cornell. For Rutgers and Cornell, this race was their historic annual Howard Smith Cup, and we were an add-on team. A typical regatta covers a 2,000-meter course in a straight path with buoyed course lanes. This type of race was different. There were two major turns in the course, so the coxswain's ability to pick a good line and point of reference to provide the pathway of least wasted strokes would be key. We looked over to the other crew teams at the start: Rutgers in their red and black, Cornell with white tank tops and red lettering. We, OSU, rocked our hunter orange with pride.

The start is a bit fuzzy. I can't recall if it was a rolling start, as many head races are, but this part doesn't matter. What does matter is that somewhere near the end of the race, as we were attempting to navigate the vital S turns toward the last 500, our stroke seat literally started having issues.

NURTURED ROWING INTENSITY

The stroke was the rower directly facing me, the coxswain, in the front of the stern of the boat. This rower is arguably the most important, as they set the tone, cadence, rhythm, stroke count, and general competitive fire for the other seven rowers that follow.

Rowing is the art of balancing power, finesse, and speed in a militaristic matching pattern. The stroke has to be on point the entire race, and the seven rowers following need to believe, mentally and physically, in the ability to vitally match power and feel throughout the entire sixty-foot shell.

Our new stroke was a sophomore named Ben, who had big shoes to fill. Our previous stroke, Nick, was an experienced stud who, pound for pound, was one of the top competitors in the nation. Nick had shared his knowledge and fiery spirit with me when I was a sophomore and junior, and now it was my turn as a senior leader to pass these qualities onto Ben, who was new to the varsity.

Ben had great length in reach and legs, and a smooth rhythm that those behind could easily follow and match. In fact, at the time his only drawback might have been his lack of ability to push the stroke rate up high enough when it was time to sprint, in part due to his gangly figure and calm and cool demeanor.

But he too was a competitor, and it was my job as the right-hand man of our coach to nurture the fire out of him and to demand every ounce of his effort through verbal assault. We had a hell of a fun time doing it... at least I did. After all, I myself had been nurtured into the figurative "mother f-er" that Coach Kjell had asked about three years previously, back at the freshman BBQ when I was still a weakling under a hundred pounds. I had a reputation for literally spitting all over my stroke, like a maddened or rabid "beaver" foaming at the mouth.

My freshman year, we raced Stanford under suave techy buildings on a man-made course in Silicon Valley. Upon crossing the finish and immediately checking the oars down to stop the boat, we gladly accepted the Cardinal jerseys off the backs of our competitors. "Tough as Nails" Travis, our bow seat, was first to cross the finish line and told it best, "I looked over to the shore and there was a dad with his hands as earmuffs over his younger daughter's head, with a look on his face as if to say, 'I can't believe I heard those words coming out of the coxswain's mouth from Oregon State.'"

The speaker system hadn't helped to muffle the vulgarity, and when one is in the zone and fully locked inside the boat, the surrounding air doesn't matter one iota. I let it all fly—no filter.

SPARKING PAST CORNELL IN TURN SPARKS CONNECTION

As we had won Stanford's jerseys my frosh year, we were determined to proudly display Cornell and Rutgers jerseys over our shoulders on the shores once our shell was tied back on our trailer that day. No stroke seat issue was going to stand in the way. So when Ben's seat started to spark (like I said, literal issues) during our power-ten move, eventually shedding one of its small wheels and creating friction, we kept going regardless

The wheels allowed Ben to smoothly slide up to the catch and roll backwards as he pressed through his legs, opened his hips, swung his body, squeezed the finish, finally cleanly feathering his oar in order to recover back up to the catch by rolling forward. The literal sparks were flying and Ben was struggling as he did this at thirty-six, then thirty-eight, then forty, then forty-two strokes per minute. Our boat continued to drive towards the finish, and we were eating seats back into Cornell and holding off the home-course host, Rutgers, who had the S-turns down pat from practiced experience. In rhythm with the drive and the run of the shell, with a muffled "huh" as the boat checked at the catch, I screamed with every muscle fiber in my chest cavity.

My abs pressing the air out of my lungs, neck veins exploding, and frothing at the mouth, I screamed, "Four seats down, now three, c'mon, fellas everything you got, break those mother f-ers, they can't hang, Cornell's fading, take it. Now we're going to go, right here, last ten—in two, one, two, you're on, ten push, nine send, eight push send, seven mooooooore, six send, (Ben looking like he might pass out, as his seat continued to spark and scream with friction) five that's it, (a wincing breath), two seats down, four more strokes, four everything you got, three one seat, two push it for each other, one dead even, last push."

At this point, a seasoned coxswain would already have their bow ball through the finish a stroke or two prior, preventing any let up as the shell cruised across the finish line. Nearly simultaneous beeps at the finish line to the boats crossing were inaudible, drowned out by the distorted speaker noise picked up through my microphone. We didn't need to hear the beeps to know we had done it, and Ben grinned. Two thousand meters, two crazy turns, a lost wheel, and we had broken through Cornell at the line to win the Howard Smith Cup by a second.

The race organizers hadn't foreseen this outcome. The cup had been perpetually passed between Rutgers and Cornell each year since the inception of the race. By jumping in to compete in a pseudo-prep race for nationals, our team had thrown a big logjam in their historical head race champion legacy. Therefore, I know we didn't go home with the Cup—I'm not sure if Cornell, by default runner-up, received it, or Rutgers as host—but it didn't matter to us. We had a jersey for each shoulder to add to our collection, a white one with red C and a red one with some oars and black R. We were on top of the world, Ben had survived, and the boat had thrived.

The actual press release from Rutgers website:

Rutgers University Athletics Heavyweight Crew Places Third in Howard Smith Cup Race Men's Rowing Posted: May 01 NEW BRUNSWICK, NJ – The Rutgers men's heavyweight varsity eight placed third behind Oregon and Cornell in the Howard Smith Cup race at the Raritan River in New Brunswick, NJ, on Saturday, May 1. The varsity team battled rough waves and strong wind conditions to finish with a time of 6:16.8, falling short of Oregon's 6:10.6. Cornell University came in second with a time of 6:11.6.

Howard Smith Cup Raritan River Cornell/ Rutgers/Oregon Varsity Eight: Oregon State 6:10.6 Cornell 6:11.6 Rutgers 6:16.8

CHAPTER TWENTY-THREE

SPARK DOMINO EFFECT

Sixteen years later, I was rummaging through my old crew jerseys from past years. I had multiple jerseys from Stanford, a proud solo Cal, a thick red Wisconsin, blue and gold Michigan and UCLA, a head race win against Yale, and there were Rutgers and Cornell. Each jersey carried a vivid memory attached to a moment in time.

The plan had been to permanently enshrine them. Through the years, I had hung them on my college bedroom wall before sending them back to my parents as I bounced around in my mid-twenties. My mom had started to cut them into squares to sew them into a quilt. In fact, the quilt backing was still in the bottom of my tattered trash bag of jerseys. But, much like an unfound book of poems by Ruhi, the quilt had never come to fruition.

So I had taken the bag of supplies, clippings, and jerseys back home with me. No better time to see this through to completion, I thought, than the global pandemic of 2020. Heck, Keena had purchased a sewing machine to start making her own cloth masks. She'd set it up in her "prepper"-style basement bedroom, along with a microwave and some snacks so she'd be able to quarantine away from me and Zu, now pushing a year old, should she be exposed to the virus.

When it comes to completing a sewing project, though, the genetic apple doesn't fall far. Those jerseys still sat, waiting to be connected together, like long-lost relatives, on a quilt of pride. Standing in our extra bedroom holding the cotton jerseys triggered memories of competitive years past.

I looked hard at the Cornell one, and was instantly back in the boat, staring at the sparks, breathlessly forcing my raspy voice to muster up energy to push back into the shell, then the mental finish line. I was still holding the red jersey with a white C—Cornell. Cornell. My mind started to drift. Cornell.

Wait, now another memory was triggered, the only other time I had even thought about this prestigious university. It all came rushing back, a second cousin and a Cornell professor. How could I not have followed up on that potential lead a few months earlier? Now, the seed was planted. When my nightly search commenced, I would follow the trail. I had an extremely outside-the-box long shot. But why not? No leaf unturned, nothing to lose.

PRAYER OF A SHOT

I had been talking with a Yifaht from Toronto. We shared 81 cM's of DNA, and she showed up as a second cousin on 23andMe. My correspondence with Yifaht K:

July 27, 2020

> **DYLAN:** Hey, how's it going? I'm trying to track down my biological father, he went by the name Ruhi. Just wanted to touch base if you might have any connection. Thanks, and take care.

> **YIFAHT:** Happy to help. What do you know about your biological father? The name Ruhi is not familiar to me at all.

> **DYLAN:** Thanks for getting back. That is really all I know. He went by "Ruhi" and was in Portland, Oregon, in 1982. In Ancestry I have an eighty-year-old relative from Milwaukee

named Beverley Cargile, she shows up as my first cousin, but I believe is my half aunt and, thus, Ruhi's half-sister. She was adopted in New York with no knowledge of family—that is why she is on Ancestry as well. Thanks for your time, Yifaht.

YIFAHT: Are you adopted as well? My father's family is from Germany, but originally from Poland. I have first cousins in Germany. My mother's family was from Poland. Both sets of grandparents moved to Israel before the Holocaust. My maternal grandmother had a brother John who survived the Holocaust and lived in New York. He was probably born in the early 1900's. That's the only relative I know of that lived in the U.S.

July 28, 2020

DYLAN: Yifaht, thanks for info. I'm not adopted, my mom just didn't have much info about him. John's an interesting lead. Upon Googling a lot of people share that name, but I can keep digging. Take care and thanks again.

YIFAHT: My mom (who lives in Israel) just told me that my dad had a relative who lived in the U.S. and was a professor at Cornell University. According to 23andMe, we are likely related through my dad's side, so John won't be so relevant to you because he's on my mom's side. Have you tried to contact RICHARD S.? He is a mutual relative of ours.

October 4, 2020

DYLAN: Appreciate the insight, I'll reach out. Thanks again. I don't see Richard as a close relative of mine... who are your closest?

Also, just curious, why do you think I'm only related on your father's side? 23andMe does not show that info for me. Do you know the last name of the Cornell professor? Thanks again for all your help, Yifaht.

My cell is 5419083039 if you want to correspond that way. I can send you a screenshot of my connections. Thanks.

Looking back now, I can't say for certain why there was a gap between July 28th and October 4th. The summer was winding down, as was my six months of daily time with Zu, who had now turned one. My usual break had been extended with the introduction of distance education due to the pandemic in the spring, and I was gearing up for an unprecedented school year in the fall of 2020.

I thought I had been meticulous over the previous two years, but here, clearly, was a stone I had left unturned. And finding it took a chance trip down memory lane, with rowing jerseys.

In reality, I think the untouched stone simply represented that, in two years, I had become more of a realist with these potential searches. I knew that our distant relationship, coupled with this random Cornell professor family member, was the longest of the long shots. This potential game-winner of prayer hoops shot wouldn't even be legal. It would need to be launched from out of bounds—from another gym, in another state. In other words, it wasn't gonna happen.

At this point, my nightly searches mostly centered on new, distant relatives that trickled in. I had resigned to playing the waiting game. My only logical hope was that an unknown close relative would take a test from one of the sites that I had been checking daily for two years. I felt like I had literally exhausted the internet and, in turn, my hope for finding Ruhi was exhausted. But, hey, resilience for Zu. Why not?

In a way, I felt numb as I sat on the couch, having tucked Zu in for the night, and reread Yifaht's message from back in July. I had not responded since July, which was uncharacteristic for me, so I responded now with appreciation and a follow-up. It was October 4th, and I figured I would share my cell number and perhaps we could text and I would be able to follow up more efficiently.

I reread her message a second time and processed. Her mom from Israel, who I assumed to be Jewish, told her that her dad had a relative in the U.S. Okay, I thought, this is why I didn't follow up. There's no chance here. This is more of a long shot than I could pose even if I tried. Furthermore, she went on to tell me that the lead, John, didn't matter anyway because he was on her mom's side.

I had become fairly savvy with the genetics game and connections by this point, and I didn't see how Yifaht would have been able to determine which side of her genome our relation manifested from. She was 99.7 percent Ashkenazi Jewish, so how could she know whether my Jewish connection was on her mom's or dad's side?

I knew she wanted to help, but like many other distant relatives I had talked with over the past years, didn't really understand how the genetic lineage game worked. Oh well, it was nice of her to at least attempt. Again, my egotistical judgement may have blinded me from the true depth of her genetic knowledge. Later, on a phone call Yifaht would share the amazing story of her adopted daughter's reconnection with her biological grand-mother using 23andMe. A lifelong of unknown separated merely by an hour's drive in the end.

WHEN I LEAST EXPECTED

The small voice from within demanded, "Follow every lead."

Without thinking much about it, numb to any sort of inner excitement after years of what felt like failure that was out of my control, I Googled, "Ruhi Cornell Professor."

Similar to thousands of searches before; the following website popped up, but missing the key "Ruhi":

Jewish Studies Affiliated Faculty - Cornell Jewish Studies

jewishstudies.cornell.edu › faculty
Jewish Studies Affiliated Faculty.

Missing: ruhi | Must include: ruhi.

I investigated the site anyway, as I always did and—nothing. Bare bones dry. So I tried clicking on the "must include: ruhi" search.

One result popped up:

Women at Cornell page 12 - eCommons@Cornell
ecommons.cornell.edu › bitstream
PDF

Cornell University, Ithaca, New York 14850. Thanks for ... years ago by a **Cornell professor** who was then, and no doubt still is, in ... 14 no. fr **RUhi** t. -444-t7M k ...

Well, I thought, if only I was looking for my biological mother instead of father. This had become a familiar song and dance. PDFs of archives, eighty-plus pages of nothing, no slivers of hope, no hints, nothing. I never stopped with just one search. It was in my nature, or nurture, to push, push, push. Rage, rage, rage.

Next search, "Ruhi Portland Oregon Cornell." Less than nothing: Neville & Butler Commercial Real Estate — Milltowner I | NEC ...

Let's simplify, I thought. I Googled "Ruhi Poet Cornell" and pressed search. Not one of my genetically crafted neurons, not one of the synaptic clefts sending motor muscle signals to the muscle fibers predisposed by heredity, believed that this pressing of my thumb might be the most significant search of my now thirty-seven years of life on this planet. Or, even more so, the most important search for my daughter's daughter's daughter as well.

I clicked search. The page loaded and up top was a Cornell.edu link:

Pretty in Pink: Grow Edible Ginger! - Cornell Small Farms
smallfarms.cornell.edu › Posts

Jan 9, 2012 — Their newly developed **Ruhi** (pronounced Rue-hee, meaning "soul" in Urdu, it is the name of a **poet** friend of Hugh's) is a selection Hugh made ...

The search summary caught my attention. This was random as hell—excited edible ginger, with the exclamation point and everything? But, as they say, the diablo is in the deets, and there was a bold "Ruhi" and bold "poet." A rare find, a very rare find.

It was like sorting through boxes of old basketball cards from the eighties and nineties., Having been shuffled through the years, their corners were tattered and random cards creased. All the good ones had been pulled out years ago and cased and traded. Deep in the pile, it looked like the edge of the famous '86-'87 Fleer set's red, blue, and white border and, at the bottom, the first name started with "Mic" and then was covered up. No way could it be a Jordan rookie, no way.

No way could it be the Ruhi poet, no way.

I pressed the link and this bad boy loaded:

Pretty in Pink: Grow Edible Ginger!
January 9, 2012/*Susan Anderson*

The sickle makes its way quickly and quietly through tall, healthy green foliage. The air smells pleasantly of ginger and earth. I hear the sound of roots giving way as Hugh Johnson and Dan Kelly pull hands of young ginger from the soil. Bright pink bud scales adorn the creamy white rhizomes of the freshly dug crop.

TRIMMING BABY GINGER TOPS.

COURTESY OF SUSAN ANDERSON.

The farm I am visiting is Puna Organics on the Big Island of Hawaii. Baby Ginger is truly beautiful in paradise but it can grow well anywhere in the United States. Hugh and Dan are growing edible ginger. It is used as a spice, a medicinal herb, and flavors many teas, drinks and confections that we commonly consume. Current scientific literature points to ginger (and turmeric, the spice high in curcumins) as having cancer-fighting properties. These properties are owed to the phytochemical compounds in ginger, namely gingerols, shogaols and zingerone, that give ginger its spicy and medicinal qualities.

BABY GINGER WITH TOPS TRIMMED.

COURTESY OF DAN KELLY.

Aside from the anticarcinogen compounds in ginger, studies have proven that ginger is effective in treating nausea, motion sickness and morning sickness. Ginger, as well as turmeric, has long been used in Ayurvedic medicine (holistic and natural medicine of Hinduism that teaches healing and prolonging of life). Both of these rhizomes are easy to grow, cultivate and market. In addition to growing and marketing mature and immature edible ginger, Puna Organics is also growing seed ginger, much to the advantage of farmers on the mainland! This seed is certified organic, disease-free and ships from the farm in Hawaii right to those who order on the mainland that want to try their hand at a phenomenal crop. Hugh and Dan are always seeking new varieties of ginger.

Their newly developed Ruhi (pronounced Rue-hee, meaning "soul" in Urdu, it is the name of a poet friend of Hugh's) is a selection Hugh made over the last 15 years of ginger from Indian origins. It initiates foliage growth quickly, makes larger rhizomes quicker and is, thus, more suited to the shorter season in the continental U.S.

SUSAN ANDERSON WITH BABY GINGER IN HAWAII.
COURTESY OF DAN KELLY.

Ruhi has the characteristic pink bud scales when harvested for baby ginger. At maturity the flesh is yellow at the growing tips with blue flesh at the base of the rhizome. Ruhi seed pieces will be readily available for the 2012 growing season. There are limited quantities of a Hawaiian yellow ginger and Thai ginger (galangal). Puna Organics also offers seed for turmeric — a variety that is robust in rhizome growth, yield, gingerols and curcumins… but that's a whole other article in itself!

Ginger in the grocery store is grown to maturity for anywhere from nine to eleven months. The ginger that we can grow in the continental United States is harvested earlier, during the young stage of rhizome growth, at about 5-8 months (referred to as Baby Ginger or young ginger).Baby Ginger is delicious! It has the characteristic bite of ginger without being hot or overpowering. The texture is akin to hearts of palm, tender yet toothsome, because the thick skin and tough fibers running through it have not yet formed. In addition to all the other things that can be done with mature ginger, immature ginger can be pickled and candied. Ginger pickles are a splendid accompaniment to Sushi, cooked greens, grilled chicken, and grains. And, last but not least, the skin accented with neon pink scales, stands out like a beacon at market!

For these reasons Baby Ginger is highly appreciated by chefs and consumers alike and commands a high price. Baby Ginger is perishable and cannot be shipped all over the world like mature ginger, but is great purchased locally. It lasts about two weeks at room temperature after being harvested, washed and trimmed. After a couple weeks it will have lost its neon look but is still fine for processing or home use. It can be frozen for later use, too. Bring frozen rhizomes out of freezer to refrigerator to thaw for use of entire rhizome; otherwise, grate frozen rhizome into recipe and put right back into the freezer.

Ginger is susceptible to some diseases and it has cultural requirements that are different from typical vegetable crops. However, once the learning curve has been surpassed, and even during, there is a sense of tropical wonder when tending this crop. It might be the smell as one walks by the plants, it could be the rhizomes peeking out of the soil surface waiting to be hilled, or the splendor of pulling something pink out of the soil could be the climax for some. For most growers, though, the reaction that they get at market, from chefs, from wholesalers, is priceless. Customers stare in awe at the pink rhizomes and ask, "Is that ginger?

HARVEƧTING BABY GINGΘR IN HAWAII
COURTEƧY OF HUGH JOHNƧON.

My visit to Puna Organics was simple — to learn the nuances of growing edible young ginger and pass it along to farmers on the mainland. Hugh Johnson has been farming organic ginger for nearly 20 years. Dan Kelly, his business partner, has been in the horticulture business for over a decade and working with Hugh for almost five years. Hugh and Dan together have forged a way to offer clean, organic ginger seed to the masses. Edible ginger is a delight; discover for yourself!

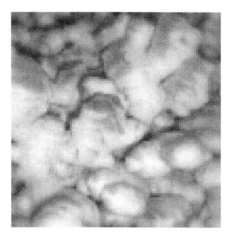

SUSAN ANDERSON

Susan Anderson owns East Branch Ginger, which represents Puna Organics on the mainland. Ginger seed pieces can be ordered from East Branch Ginger's website eastbranchginger. com or by calling 207-313-4358. Seed is shipped directly from the Big Island of Hawaii right to your door.

CHAPTER TWENTY-FOUR

THE CYCLE OF LIFE ON THE BIG ISLAND

Random? No, even more than random. A ginger root farm on the Big Island of Hawaii. Back in January 2015, I had visited the Big Island solo.

Keen and I had been mobilized as nurses with the Army Reserve to Tripler Army Medical Hospital on Oahu for six months. Responsible Keen hung tight on our short two days off to work on her doctorate studies. She had been fighting to keep up on top of the sixty-plus hours of nursing shifts we had been filling.

Always up for an adventure and looking to maximize experience, I "island hopped" a short flight to the Big Island. I had more greens in my pocket than I had in 2006, when I first lived in Hawaii as a grad assistant hoops coach, and I'd always wanted to check out the largest—and still growing—active volcanic island in the chain.

I rented a small car that I slept in, and zipped around the entire coastline. I hit black sanded beaches of igneous rock broken down by ocean waves, then the famous cattle Parker Ranch, and onto Hawaii Volcanoes National Park, where I hiked the lava tubes and took in the soft glow over the open earth where magma flowed below. And, the highlight, I hiked up Mauna Loa Observatory next to snowboard tracks and toured the telescopes, followed by a night of stargazing.

Maybe I slept in the car next to the ginger root farm. Or maybe not. Either way it would have been less random than this parenthesized line midway through an article from 2012, which had nothing to do with a potential relative professor from Cornell. It was just simply posted in the Cornell Small Farms Program online op-ed from the ag and life science department. In some ways I'm surprised, looking back, that I made it through the entire article to find the needle. So small a chance, so random a connection, but there it was:

> Their newly developed Ruhi (pronounced Rue-hee, mean-
> ing "soul" in Urdu, it is the name of a poet friend of Hugh's) is
> a selection Hugh made over the last 15 years of ginger from
> Indian origins.

RANDOM CHANCE, PURE LUCK, OR DESTINED FATE

To think that without Susan, the author, deciding to include that the ginger was named after Hugh's friend, my Google search would not have hit. Furthermore, her decision to mention Ruhi's name and go as far as to define and pronounce it in parentheses, and then to describe him as a friend and poet is what placed this article on top of my browser.

This single article about ginger rose to the top of over four billion web pages that were searched for the simple, yet indispensable, three words: "Ruhi Poet Cornell." This coupled with the random coincidence that it happened to be a Cornell publication. Even though Yifaht's potential lead of a family professor had absolutely nothing to do with this article, it was the exact linchpin required to produce the search.

This serendipity—or, perhaps, fate—was like pulling out an entire box of Jordan rookie cards all cased and in mint condition that were covering up a 1909 Honus Wagner, the most valuable baseball card of all. That level of fortuitousness, and that lucky.

Or maybe not. I really had nothing concrete yet, just a random reference to a poet who went by Ruhi and had a friend with a ginger root farm on the Big Island. But hey, who was I if not someone unafraid to push? It was within me, be it nature or nurture. It was my defining flaw and characteristic. So push I would.

NEXT MOVE: RIDE THE WAVE

Recalibrating facts, what I had was the contact information for the woman who wrote the article eight long years earlier. I imagined the cascade of things that could have changed in nearly a decade: the name of the ginger farm, the name of the farmer himself, Hugh, who is mentioned to be a friend of this "Ruhi" poet, and the name of Hugh's business partner.

I hit the ground rolling, sending out late-night emails to all of the above. I found a personal website from Hugh where he'd posted info about motorcycle riding and events on the Big Island dated over the past ten years, but it seemed to be dormant. I found a contact for his business buddy, but from what also looked like a cold website.

Nevertheless, in two years I had become a humbled crackerjack in tracking people down via the web and was able to find a reference to Hugh's lady friend, Elvira, on a broken website thread. With that nugget, I parlayed the connection into a bed and breakfast website that looked legit: Your Hawaiian Retreat, owned by Elvira. It was alive and it had a contact icon.

Click, and there was a contact form. I wasn't overly confident, but had absolutely nothing to lose. This was the first warm lead I had in nearly a year, so I was diving in without hesitation, whether or not I was wearing board shorts and "slippahs," whether or not the Hawaiian sea urchins would reignite our longtime reef rivalry—didn't matter.

STRANGERƨ HELPING STRANGERƨ

I submitted my contact at 5 p.m., and also shot off a handful of emails to all of the other contacts I could find surrounding Hugh and the article, including his business partner, Daniel:

On Sun, Oct 4, 2020 at 5:49 PM
Name: **DYLAN MORO**
Email Address: dylan.moro@k12.sd.us

> Accommodation: Any / Other
>
> Message: Hi, awesome place. Contacting to follow up about poet friend Ruhi? My cell is 5419083039 thank you
>
> (*Sent via Your Hawaiian Retreat*)

On *Mon, Oct 5, 2020 at 11:24 AM* **MORO, DYLAN** <Dylan.Moro@k12.sd.us> wrote:

> Long story short, biker dude Hugh Johnson mentions Ruhi got its name from a poet friend of the same name. I am searching for my biological father, who went by Ruhi and was a poet in Portland, Oregon, 1982. Any help is much appreciated, thanks for your time,
>
> Dylan

By 11 p.m., I heard back from Hugh's business partner:

On *Oct 4, 2020, at 10:44 PM,* **HOG GINGER** <orderhogorder@gmail.com> wrote:

> I have forwarded your email to Hugh, AKA Biker Dude.
>
> Best, -d

And by 1 a.m., I had a response from Hugh himself:

Mon 10/5/2020 12:59 AM

Hi Dylan,

I just heard from Ruhi recently. He is in Florida. His given name, I think, is Marc Frank. I imagine Ruhi is mid to late seventies. I could email him with your info if you like and you can go from there.

I do not think I have seen Ruhi for about eight years. We touch base from time to time. So please keep in touch. Meanwhile, I'll let Ruhi know you asked and will give him your email address.

Aloha,
Hugh

MOMENTS OF EMOTION, THE WAIT IS THE HARDEST PART

It was 1 a.m. and I was now wired. Fortunately, my wide-awakeness paired well with Zu in the rocking chair, where she was fighting through another sleepless night. Not only were we getting in some good bonding time, but it would potentially score me some points with Keen if I was the one hanging through the night for a change while she caught some z's.

My mind tossing in the undertow, I looked at Zu's face and zoned out. Everything filtered through the question of, what if? I had to temper expectations, to relax. There are probably hundreds of poets with the pen name Ruhi. What made this one special?

I looked down on Zu again. Her eyes were now closed, so I placed her in her crib and tried to uncover anything I could by Googling "Marc Frank," "Marc Ruhi Frank," "Marc Ruhi Frank Poet." While typing in these searches, my mom's words from a while back slammed me: two first names.

This wasn't Lawrence Martin, but it was two first names. In that moment, I froze—this seemed to be a secondary verification, a faint and embryonic one, but developing legs. How much life to give it? I need not wait long.

I was reading up on the Cuban author Marc Frank, modestly thinking, could this be the dude? Doesn't seem to fit. It was 3 a.m. and Zu had been resting for a solid hour when an email came in on my phone. I caught the sender's name as the window up top popped in on my phone, marcruhifrank8@gmail.com:

MARC FRANK <marcruhifrank8@gmail.com>
Mon 10/5/2020 3:23 AM

Dear Dylan,

I received an email from my friend Hugh Johnson on the Big Island Hawaii. Something about biological father. I couldn't understand Hugh's email.

Yes, I was given the pen name Ruhi & some friends call me Ruhi.

If you like, you can email me & explain yourself.

Ruhi

I couldn't type fast enough, but tried to remain calm and stay in somewhat speculative, investigative mode. Yet, I wanted to believe. If my Ruhi was a wandering poet nearly forty years ago, would he have a Gmail account in 2020?

I shot an email back. It was now 4 a.m. Zu was starting to toss a bit.

MORO, DYLAN
Mon 10/5/2020 4:03 AM

Hi Marc/Ruhi,

Thank you very much for being willing to correspond. Quite a long shot, but after doing 23andMe and AncestryDNA, I found out I am genetically half Jewish. The man who raised me, John Moro, is not. Here's what I know from my mom, Debra Moro (Brink).

Ruhi was a partner of hers on the southern Oregon coast in 1982. I believe him to now be in his seventies. They met on a bus in Portland, Oregon, and he was/is a poet who gave her a poetry book he penned titled *Petals of Light*. They went to a Guru Maharaj Ji enlightenment group together. She thinks he may have been from the East Coast and was a traveler, but she did not know his surname.

My closest Jewish relative is a woman named Beverly Cargile, who I think is my half aunt and a half sibling of Ruhi, she lives in Milwaukee and was adopted in a closed adoption from the East Coast with no info of family name. Like I said, probably a coincidence and long shot, but I read an article about a ginger root named after a poet buddy named Ruhi and thought I'd do my due diligence as two years has produced no real leads. Take care and thanks for your time,

J Dylan Moro , my cell is 5419083039

Sent from my iPhone

I waited for a bit, now up cuddling Zu again. Half an hour passed and in comes a response email:

Mon 10/5/2020 4:35 AM

Hi Dylan,

I think you're looking for another Ruhi, for all that you mention I don't recall, especially the Guru.

I was in the Pacific Northwest in the eighties & I am in my seventies.

I'm sorry it's not me, for I can understand your wish to make contact with your biological father. I do hope you're able to find him.

Marc/Ruhi

THE DARKNESS BETWEEN FIREFLIES

A familiar numbness returned. I immediately re-read his words. Name? Check. Poet? Check. Pacific Northwest in the eighties? Check. Age? Check.

As I was processing and reading my phone, Keen made her way downstairs. I followed her down, carrying Zu, and started to explain, interrupted by an incoming call. It was just shy of 5 a.m. I passed Zu to Keen and opened the sliding glass door to the early-morning darkness on our back deck, with town lights glowing below and the Black Hills silhouetted to the southwest. I answered the call.

"Hi, this is Dylan."

A soft, slow, genuine voice on the other side said, "Hello, Dylan, this is Ruhi. I received your message from my friend Hugh."

Everything I was doing and thinking slowed down to match his vocal cadence. His stroke rate was leisurely at best.

"I am sorry to say, but I am not the Ruhi you are searching for."

My mom was a talker, I was a talker, but in this moment, I listened. My mind, typically racing, seemed to have a singular focus, to patiently hear and be present with the elderly sounding man on the phone. He went on, "I have no memory of your mother or the story you described, I'm sorry. It's not me."

I heard his words, but I wasn't convinced. In fact, the more he spoke, the more and more his voice, cadence, audible demeanor, and the manner in which he was navigating the phone call seemed to match the description of the man I had built in my mind.

I had constructed a mental image based upon numerous conversations with my mom, where I had asked her to describe anything she could remember about him. Her lack of details, strangely, seemed to epitomize the voice I was hearing and, even more so, the spirit of which was producing the sound. Or perhaps I was naively filling in the cracks in a self-serving, excessively hopeful manner. Attempting to fire my game-winning buzzer beater.

Our connection seemed intrinsic, though. I had made instant connections with others at different times in my life. I thought of my pops and I imprinting on each other floating in the tub, my cousin Brando in our early youth stomping through the woods, my best man will on summer forest service truck rides, my sister Jer while sharing ice cream cones dressed as clowns, my bro Julio while playing NBA Jam, my youngest sister Lena when she was born at home and it was my role to say if it was a boy or girl and then later hiking through the Alp's of Austria together, my mom taking a sandy toe barefoot walk on shore acre's beach heading towards the perfect tide pool bowls to search for sea critters, Con at OSU, Keen on the sand volley court at DWU, Zu holding and counting her toes for the first time while an exhausted and courageous Keen smiled up at us. The more this Ruhi denied our connection, the more my neural cells seemed to conjecture the contrary. A human may attempt to control one's own mind, but intuition can overwhelm seeming authority. My mind was "whelmed." Not over, just the amount to stay calm and reply.

"Okay, well I appreciate you responding and calling me."

Ruhi then went on, "I lived in the Pacific Northwest, but I just have no memory of your mother. When I was a boy in Paris, I heard a voice tell me, 'Marc, do not have close relations with women,' but I am saddened to say I didn't listen. I should have, but I didn't. I understand wanting to have a father in your life. It seems as you had a man raise you?"

"Yes, my dad, John, is a great man. I've been very fortunate."

I was processing his Paris story and questioning his need to confess to promiscuity, but it did not bother me. I felt slowed-down and focused as I leaned against the deck railing in the early fall morning breeze.

"I am happy you had a father, I know people that never had a positive male figure in their lives."

"Yes, having a daughter now, I have a firsthand account of the important bond between parents and kids."

As we continued to talk, it wasn't so much the subject matter, but the rhythm and tempo of our conversation forming a connection I felt physically. I wondered if he did as well. The more he talked, numerous times denying that he could be the Ruhi I had been searching for over the past two years, the more I felt that he might be the Ruhi. I understood this was irrational, but my gut, my heart, my mind were all aligning. It wasn't what he was saying, but the way he said it.

"Well, I am happy that you have a loving family. You seem to have a good life."

"Ya, I do. I appreciate you being willing to correspond. Whether you are the Ruhi I've been searching for or not, it was good to visit with you."

I genuinely meant it. We had been talking for a half hour or so, and I felt calm and balanced. I felt an unadulterated sense of kindness in this moment, a feeling I'd experienced throughout my life with various amounts of sincerity. My emotions were satisfied. Could it be the start to the end of my adventure? My intuitions said yes—even though this journey centered on one other human, too, and he happened to disagree. It didn't matter. I was resilient, respectful, and confident.

We ended the call with well wishes and I walked back inside to my Keena and Zuzu.

"Was that him?" Keen asked.

"I don't know," was my logical answer. "He says no, but I think maybe? In fact, the longer we talked the more certain I felt."

"Wow. What are you going to do now?"

I gave Zu a kiss and Keen a side hug.

"I s'pose I'll talk to Deb, and go from there."

I'm sure Keena could tell I wasn't going to give up at this point. I would exhaust all angles. I had slayed the internet, but I would try to maintain respect and tact. I would use a gentle push—if such a thing existed. It was my nature to pursue fact and truth, a tendency that was also nurtured.

NEXT LOGICAL STEPS

I sent a follow-up email back to Marc:

> Thank you, Marc, for corresponding. It was great to visit with
> you this morning. Here is a picture of me and my family, my
> wife Keena and daughter Zuzu. My mother Debra's number is
> 5412XXXX06 and her email is doodles_@hotmail.com. I will fill
> her in today. Take care and have a great day,
>
> Dylan

When I got to school, I checked and had received an email back. I had an almost giddy feeling throughout the morning:

MARC FRANK <marcruhifrank8@gmail.com>
Mon 10/5/2020 5:40 AM

> Thank you too, Dylan. Lovely family you have. Don't have a photo but shall ask someone to take a picture.
>
> Marc/Ruhi
>
> I shall forward you a work titled *Clouds of Light* published at Portland State University by professor friends at the time. Wrote it in the early sixties, beginning in Israel & wrote out traveling overland to India.

I forwarded all emails on to my mom, and shot Ruhi back:

> Thanks, Marc/Ruhi, and sounds good, I look forward to reading your poetry. Take care.

And got back: "Most welcome, be well!"

I also received and wrote back to Hugh:

> Aloha, thanks so much for helping to connect. Had a good conversation with Ruhi, he seems to be a truly kind man. Keep you posted on details.
>
> Much mahalo,
>
> Dylan
>
> *Sent from my iPhone*

On Oct 6, 2020, at 1:33 AM

Hey Dylan, hope you find your daddy.

Aloha, Hugh

LISTEN TO MEMORY

I called my mom during my first break at school and attempted to convey everything that had happened in the past twelve hours or so. I shared the story of the ginger root article, and explained that I'd contacted a man who went by Ruhi. I forwarded her the email he had sent, denying that he was the Ruhi, and attempted to recite the phone call we shared.

Her response was, as always, kind and respectful but presenting me with the facts.

"D, if he says he's not the Ruhi, you may need to listen to his words."

I knew she was right, but the righteous, stubborn competitor in me couldn't help but push back. I finally felt like I was on the precipice of closure.

"Ya, s'pose so," a phrase that usually indicates the start of an unrelenting sarcastic line, "there were probably a dozen-plus poets with the pen name Ruhi wandering around Portland in the early eighties. But Mom, you should hear his voice, his cadence, it seems vividly familiar. Maybe because of the way you have described him, but I don't know, it just fits. You should talk to him, and see what you think."

I was in my natural form here. I was pushing another person into a potentially uncomfortable situation, for my own selfish reasons, and not feeling any aversion to doing it. She paused on the other side. I started to question why I hadn't locked down some details. Was he a traveler? It seemed like he was, and he had spoken of some spiritual groups he had attended in the University of Portland area, but denied specifically seeing the Guru Maharaj Ji my mom had cited.

My younger mind was attempting to connect fuzzy memories between two older people who were once connected for a moment in time, but had spent lives growing further apart each day. Both of them seemed to be in denial of what I was starting to peg as a certain truth. Pump the brakes, I told myself. Perhaps I was actively over-forcing the square peg.

"Would you be willing to talk with him on the phone? I can connect you two in a three-way call."

She calmly said, "Let me think about it, maybe give me a day or so to consider it."

Here I was again, forcing others to reconcile choices they had made and asking them to explore past memories that may have faded for purposeful reasons.

"OK, Mom, sounds good, I love you. Thanks for everything and have a good day. Say hi to Johnny. You can share any or all with him, of course."

"Love you, Dylan, all will be as it should. He does have two first names."

Yes, he does, I thought. With so many details flooding at once, it was hard to keep on top of the information being presented. I had years to process what little I had initially known, and now it seemed like minutes or seconds between giant dominoes falling. Or was I just imagining their connections to one another, continuing the path to a central truth? If Marc "Ruhi" Frank was the central domino, he was steadfast in his certainty that he was not to fall in place. He was certain it was not him.

I felt confidence in the sentiment that a voice can trigger memory. If Deb and Marc heard each other's voices, might they hear familiarity—even more so than they might recognize faces aged forty years. Perhaps it was all in the voice. I thought back to the call I had with Marc. He had apologized that he'd been a user of European tobacco, so his voice was distorted a bit. I had made clear to him that I thought he had a kind-sounding voice. Might my mom recognize it? I'd soon find out.

CHECK THE RECORD

We shared this chain of emails throughout the morning:

MARC FRANK <marcruhifrank8@gmail.com>
Mon 10/5/2020 6:15 AM

Gulf of Mexico

MORO, DYLAN

Mon 10/5/2020 7:14 AM

To: Marc Frank <marcruhifrank8@gmail.com>

Awesome picture, Marc, looks like a great spot. It's an interesting game, looking for physical similarities... Thank you again for being willing to talk. I imagine you don't have a picture from your younger years? I am looking forward to my mom checking out the picture and poetry. My mind draws similarities to both to your shoulders and legs. Enjoy the day, we'll be in touch,

Dylan

EYES

Then there are the eyes. Dad and all of my siblings have such an intolerance to sunlight they develop an alter-ego state that we've affectionately named "Squinty." This state occurs in blinding sunlight, of course. Even in mild exposure, they reflexively squint in the minimal light and physically nod their heads as if to cower away from the light. I have never experienced this phenomenon. For the rest of my family, sunglasses are a life raft or a misery, while I wear shades as much for looks as for practicality.

I took art in high school and was sketching one lazy Sunday. Johnny was stretched out on the couch. I was a D-plus artist at best, but drawing his facial profile was gratifying. Even with his eyes closed behind his glasses, his large ocular cavities and long eyelashes were undeniably his most distinguishing qualities. My sisters, Jer and Deebs, had long received the same compliments about their big eyes.

In fact, Jerri had the disturbing party trick of being able to protrude her eyes to make it seem like they were literally out of their sockets, a creepy and funny skill that I couldn't even dream of mimicking. My bro Julian's big eyes made him the most obliterated victim of the "squint." (Just to prove I've still got it in the fearless eye-to-sun ballgame, I recently spun the bike up Lookout Mountain on a sunny sixty-degree day. No shades and no squint.)

WORM LOOKƒ

I started venturing down the wormhole of what it meant, anyway, to look like someone. People who have spent years and years together sometimes seem to take on a similar look. Older couples carry themselves with similar gaits. In some strange sense, it's as if they are truly rubbing off on each other.

We use the term "bowsers" from a favorite movie, *I Love You, Man*, about humans that look like their dogs and vice-versa. Perhaps it's just random coincidence, but there seems to be something innate in how physical manifestations arise in humans based on their environment, personal preferences, or intent to physically present themselves in a certain way.

Mon 10/5/2020 7:15 AM

To: Marc Frank <marcruhifrank8@gmail.com>

Sent from my iPhone

MARC FRANK <marcruhifrank8@gmail.com>
Mon 10/5/2020 8:31 AM

To: Moro, Dylan

Sorry, Dylan, don't have any other photos. Oh, just remembered another picture on some writing, taken in North Carolina. Shall see if I can find it.

Marc or Ruhi

MARC FRANK <marcruhifrank8@gmail.com>
Mon 10/5/2020 8:58 AM

To: Moro, Dylan

Sorry, Dylan, don't remember your mother looking at photo.

MORO, DYLAN
Mon 10/5/2020 9:00 AM

To: Marc Frank <marcruhifrank8@gmail.com>

No worries, and thanks again for looking. I'll try and find an older picture of her as well. Keep you posted

MARC FRANK <marcruhifrank8@gmail.com>
Mon 10/5/2020 9:02 AM

> To: Moro, Dylan

> Thank you, please do. I don't tend to keep photos of myself, just poems & pieces.

MORO, DYLAN
Mon 10/5/2020 11:23 AM

> To: Marc Frank <marcruhifrank8@gmail.com>

> Here's a younger picture. She went by Debbie. Thanks again.

Sent from my iPhone

MARC FRANK <marcruhifrank8@gmail.com>
Mon 10/5/2020 2:33 PM

> To: Moro, Dylan

> Thank you! Your mother emailed.

I followed up with Ruhi on a few different leads I thought might have some viability. Years previously, upon digging for information about Janice W., I had found her mother's short obituary note with family names and contacts. I slipped the text of the obituary into an email to Ruhi without any detailed explanation.

MORO, DYLAN
Mon 10/5/2020 11:28 AM

> To: Marc Frank <marcruhifrank8@gmail.com>

> Do any of these family names seem familiar?

> **BUSH**
> Frances (nee Elkin), age 94 passed away peacefully on December 19, 2011. Beloved wife of the late (1987) Sam. Loving mother of Marcelle, Janice and Allan. Devoted grandmother of five and cherished great grandmother of six. Funeral arrangements entrusted to Jewish Memorial Chapel - Clifton, NJ. A Chapel Service will take place today at 11:30 AM with interrment to immediately follow at Beth El Cemetery in Washington Township, NJ. www.jewishmemorialchapel.org

> **Jewish Memorial Chapel**
>
> The Jewish Memorial Chapel is a unique funeral home. It is one of only a few nonprofit funeral homes in the United States. The Chapel is owned and operated by the Synagogues and other Jewish organizations in the area.
>
> www.jewishmemorialchapel.org

Also do you have siblings, or any other children? What were your parents' names, or uncles/aunts? Appreciate any info, just trying to piece together potential.

MARC FRANK <marcruhifrank8@gmail.com>
Mon 10/5/2020 2:46 PM

To: Moro, Dylan

Yes, they are family on my mother's side.

Marc/Ruhi

Not only had he recognized the names, but he confirmed my hunch by claiming they were on his mother's side. His positive identification offered me a back door into our genetic connection. Now I had a strong piece of tangible evidence that pushed me into 99 percent certainty range that I had found the Ruhi I was looking for, whether he believed so or not.

Janice showed up as my close Jewish relative through Ancestry DNA, so if, in fact, these were his relatives on his mother's side, then the proof was evident. I had long moved past my skepticism over the tests' accuracy. The science was there, as proven by all of my known family members who had populated on my maternal side. Ironically, the person I'd tried to contact as my original, primary lead, Janice, proved to be the linchpin—with or without her active help.

I could see the physical similarities between us as well. I saw my legs in his photo, along with my weak, slightly hunched, shoulder frame. Heck, the dude even had my clothing style—including the exact same Chaco sandals I sported on hikes.

Now my task seemed to be to persuade the two humans who could certify this connection, the creators, Deb and Ruhi. They both had nebulous memories of the past. Ruhi had immediately denied the potential he was my father. Well, I thought, let's get them on the phone together and sit back and see what happens. If a portion of this was about adventure, how many thirty-seven-year-old adults have the opportunity to reconnect their biological parents after nearly forty years? That sounds like an adventure anyone would want, right?

Or maybe it was just the plight of a pushy, half Jewish weakling who found it hard to take no for an answer.

I talked with my mom again later on. She decided she'd give it a day. I was supposed to check back the next day and see if she might be willing to talk on the phone with Ruhi. I backed off the pushing and agreed, recognizing they both needed to be on board.

I did share with her the nugget about him recognizing the family names I'd found through the Ancestry-Janice connection, but I wasn't sure if she completely understood what I was trying to convey. I tried to simplify, saying I was 99 percent sure he was the correct Ruhi, even though he didn't believe so.

"I think if we all got on the phone together, the truth might work itself out."

"Okay, D, let me think about it some more."

Even my non-pushing was pushy.

After receiving his email about recognizing the family names, I replied to Marc at the end of the school day:

MORO, DYLAN
Mon 10/5/2020 3:38 PM

> To: Marc Frank <marcruhifrank8@gmail.com>

> That's very interesting. Let me know if you'd be willing to or have some time to talk on the phone later, Marc. I appreciate it, take care.

CHAPTER TWENTY-FIVE

SIT BACK AND LISTEN

The next morning came and I called Ruhi, asking if he would be willing to visit with Debra, as well, if I added her on the call. He said, "That is fine, Dylan."

I called Debra, and told her that Marc was on the other line and willing to talk with both of us. This was not me being pushy, it was just a straight-up trap. I knew I was being terribly manipulative.

She said, "Okay, D, if he is willing."

I merged the calls, let Marc know Debra was on the other line, and sat down to listen for a change. Debra is a great conversationalist, especially with strangers and the elderly. She kindly introduced herself, thanked him for being willing to talk with the two of us, and started in on the story she recalled. He listened, and when she finished, just stated, "I'm sorry, Debra, but I don't remember you."

You could hear the age and kindness in his soft, slow voice. I made the mental connection, he sounded like a sleepy Clarence from *It's a Wonderful Life*. The movie was a favorite for both Keen's family and mine growing up, and it was where we had gleaned Zu's namesake, Zuzu's petals. Zuzu's petals, the evanescent poem book *Petals of Light* by Ruhi—the connections and coincidences were piling up. Or, perhaps, I was just leaning in completely, and allowing myself to become overly aware of them.

At this moment, Debra mentioned the poem book he had gave her back in the early eighties. "The Ruhi I had come to know shared a book of poems with me. It was called *Petals of Light*. I have told Dylan that I would find it, and have been searching over the past two years, but am yet to uncover it."

If eye rolling was audible, they might have both heard me. But at this moment, they both tipped their hands more obviously than at any other time. Neither of them could accurately remember the poem book, which gave me some insight into the fuzzy nature of the whole encounter.

Neither of them recognized what they were doing, but from Debra's tone of voice my intuition told me she was sensing a level of familiarity in his vocal cadence. And when she mentioned the book, Ruhi said, "Yes, Debra, if you are able to find this book of poems, I am sure this would be the connection of proof."

I attempted to use sound science to reconcile their positions with my own logical mindset. I had studied science throughout my post-secondary education—general-sci, bio, and then nursing. For the past two years, I had learned all that I could about genetics and family lineage, statistics of percentage of relations, chromosome cM's, and geographical genetic lineage. I now fully believed in the science behind the genetic tests. A poem book from thirty-seven years ago was somewhat arbitrary to me at this point. For me, the book was something I could have used during the previous two years to help in searching. But for Marc and Debra, it was a shared physical token they could both rest their minds upon, and I could respect that. I could see how their minds were struggling to corroborate their actual time together, and the specific time that my life was created and came to exist in this world.

'IT' SKIPS A GENERATION

I could remember the exact moment that Keen and I had decided to try starting a family. We were in our mid-thirties, had stable careers, had moved into our second home, and had recently become veterans after being honorably discharged from the Army Reserve. Our life together seemed solid, and we felt ready and excited.

Debra and Marc needed a lost poetry book that he didn't recall writing, and she hadn't seen for who knows how long. They hadn't been able to manifest and certify the connection via a phone call, but all I needed was science, via a tube of saliva.

Mom continued her story, telling about the black DeSoto she had borrowed from her brother to drive to the coast with the Ruhi she had known. I continued to sit back as Marc denied remembering. Debra's Ruhi had taken the bus down south from Portland. Marc stumbled through, saying that he remembered a Debra from northern California. This was an obvious connection in my mind, as North Bend/Coos Bay was but a couple hours from the California border. Again, their combined recollection of that time seemed fuzzy at best.

PATIENT PATIENT

It was starting to become mildly painful for me to not interject. Here's what was running through my head:

Listen, guys, it's both of you. Ruhi, you yourself recognized the familial names from a proven genetic relative, which is the closest proof I can get without a blood or saliva sample. Also, Debra, perhaps he isn't perfectly picking up on your vividly clear recollection because you yourself and your story may have some inaccuracies. Remember how you originally thought both Ruhi and Trish had left this earth?

Marc, do you think it might be a strange coincidence that you were close with another Debra in "Northern California"? And when you visited her, you say, you were on a bus rolling south from P-town? Furthermore, you might have a slight amount of logistical inaccuracy based on the lifestyle you were living and this having been nearly forty years ago.

Was I taking crazy pills here? It was the early eighties in Portland, Oregon, and you both were, in your minds, attending different spiritual enlightenment groups—heck, let's call a spade a spade, these seemed more like cult-like hippy gatherings—in the same location at the same time. And NEITHER OF YOU CAN BE CERTAIN THE OTHER IS THE PERSON THAT I HAVE WORKED TIRELESSLY FOR TWO YEARS TO BLEEPING CONNECT, WITHOUT A NAME OR LOCATION? Are you kidding me?

I took a breath. I was still sitting quietly and not interjecting, with a slight smile. I had the foresight and peace of mind to sit back and let it unfold as it may, as I already felt confident in my research. At that moment, it wasn't me who needed to say anything. My mom took the reins, as she often does in conversation. In a warm and kind fashion, she simply posed, "Ruhi or Marc, I'm not sure what to call you. What would you like to be referred to as?"

He answered in a soft, accepting, and higher-pitched voice. "Either is fine, Debra, I have been called both throughout my life. I was given Marc as a child, and through my writing I was given the pen name Ruhi and now also 'Ruki Rumi.'"

He went into great depths explaining his names, and also reciting the voice in Paris he had wished he had listened to, the one that demanded he avoid close relations with women.

RЄAL TIMЄ NATURЄ VS. NURTURЄ

I settled back into my strong opinion. Well, dude, I'm glad you didn't avoid women. I wouldn't be here if you had. After he finished, ten minutes of explanation later, it was clear where I had gotten my tendency for breathless, run-on sentence stories, wearing others out with my relentless ability to steal the oxygen out of the room. As Keen would put it, lovingly, I "never allow others to get a word in."

This was clearly nature, with a bit of modeling from Deb. On the other hand, Johnny nurtured the quiet side. In fact, Jer and I often joked that if we wanted to have a full convo with Johnny, we should call him from the other room. He was a different dude on the telephone than in person. My pops and I could spend a weekend hiking through the Wallowa mountains and share a few deep talks over the course of a few minutes. But we could go an hour straight on the phone, from weather, to hiking, to biking, to hoops, to politics, religion, to the problems with the healthcare system, the mistreatment of Native Americans, big oil conspiracies, the "truth" about the wealthy and what the government wanted of poor people. We could talk about his travels through Europe, the book he had been reading about Antarctic exploration or a trip through South America, the movie he had watched about the Pyramids, his shooting percentage in his weekly pickup hoops games, the guitar solo he had mastered for the third band he was filling in with, the fact that this was the most extreme snow or sun he had ever experienced in all of his life, how much the weather was changing on this world and what we were or weren't doing about it, how beautiful the hike he took up to Slick Rock was, and how many morels he had scored on his last hunt near Fergie. How lame the people of Los Angeles were, how beautiful his home area in Oregon was and why wouldn't anybody choose to live there? Followed closely by, there are too many tourists this summer and why is everyone starting to move to Joseph? 'I mean, the trails are crazy overrun, Dylan, you wouldn't believe it—it's unbelievable,' the delicious pie or bread he had been laboring over, how great his garden was coming along, if he could keep the deer out of it.

All of these topics were linked with cute, kind, nervous giggling. I knew my dad, and I knew him well. He was my lifelong best friend.

NURTURED EXTREME AND CONNECTION

Aristotle said, "There is no great genius without some touch of madness."

During his Euro tripping, Johnny had been called "Madman Moro." He was dubbed as such in congruence with his fearless ability to conquer the physical. He would run twenty-plus miles, jump into the Running of the Bulls in Pamplona, and climb Hahns Peak during family reunions as others found a lounger and a brew.

I loved this about my pops as I walked closely behind him in the summer of 2020, summiting Dollar Peak in the Wallowa Mountains. I braced myself against the steep drop-off, ready to be able to push him back up the slope should his sixty-nine years of physicality momentarily let him down. I had looked to find some calm and quiet while reconnecting with my pops, and we set out on the hike from a different access point than usual, Tenderfoot Trail, to avoid summer crowds.

Oftentimes the trail and the woods were the places to interact with him. It's where we could share connection, advice, and stories. On this trip, besides prioritizing mosquito avoidance and drinking in the 360 degrees of alpine scenery, most importantly we had time together.

LOVE AND FAITH DURING ADVERSITY

In 2007, Keen and I were home for holiday break from nursing school when my dad started coughing up blood and falling to the floor.

He was transferred to Walla Walla, Washington, a few days later, where physicians made it clear that there was nothing more they could do for him. They advised us that, should we head west and show up at the ER, Oregon Health and Science University would not be able to turn away treatment for my uninsured pops. Not exactly the most confident situation a family might wish to find themselves when a life hangs in the balance, but we all kept optimism and hope as we drove dated vehicles 250 miles in winter weather.

The front passenger seat of the hand-me-down Honda was broken, in a permanent state of recline, which served fine for my pops to try to rest in. A doc in Walla Walla had a professional relationship with a cancer surgeon back in Portland, where our story as a family had started, and he thought he may be able to help.

I sat, and slept, in the bedside hospital lounger next to him on the same OHSU campus where, ten years previously, I had my growth hormones checked. We cracked jokes about the flying alien bacon in an original, late-night *Star Trek* episode. It wasn't quite the *Next Generation* quality that we had shared as a family during the nineties, but it provided temporary comedic relief.

His chest tube canister filled up a bit more with each wheeze of laughter, ultimately totaling seven liters of serosanguinous drainage from the volleyball-sized tumor entangling his spleen. To treat his freshly diagnosed, stage-four Non-Hodgkin's Lymphoma, he started a heavy regiment of R CHOP chemotherapy and a new study drug trial, Enzastaurin.

I didn't fear his death. I felt confidence and strength in his ability to fight and survive. It may have been out of ignorance, but I also felt a great deal of appreciation for the quality time we had already had together.

Perhaps for this reason, two-plus years later the moment at our wedding that I was overcome with emotion (ducking my head behind Keen to mask tears) was when he was on the microphone sharing loving words with Keen and I, our families surrounding, as a cancer survivor.

He stated later, as the lone recovered case of his trial, that it was music, the outdoors, and love of family and friends that healed him, keeping alive his spirit and will to live. The chemo couldn't have hurt. Nature's beauty and calm serve to restore and provide a place where we continue to feel spiritual connection, in awe of God's or Yahweh's works.

DEBRA CUTS TO THE CHASE

Back on the phone call with Ruhi, my mom was about to put the nail in the coffin of doubt, at least for me. These two might continue to speculate until the book of poems was found. Regardless, without hesitation or being preemptively prompted, after Ruhi had finished his ten-minute recounting of his past history, she said, "Ruhi, might you be willing to take a genetic test like the one Dylan took—when he found out he was indeed half Jewish?"

Without much pause and with slow, patient cadence in soft voice, he responded, "That would be fine, Debra, if that is what Dylan wishes I would be willing to give blood or whatever was needed."

"I think all you need is to spit in a tube, isn't that right, D?"

They remembered I was on the call. Cool.

"Yes, that's all it would take, and I could have a kit sent directly to you, Ruhi, and set up all of the information so all you would need to do is put it in the mail. It's a pretty simple process. I just would need your address."

As I spoke, it was clear I was mirroring Ruhi's slow pace and also Debra's vocal rate and flow. I knew the more I could take care of the details, the more smoothly this would go.

"That would be fine, Dylan, I will share my address with you through email. I think that is all for now."

"Yes, thank you, Marc or Ruhi, it was great to talk with you, and thank you for being willing to help Dylan with this quest. He has been searching for some time now."

"Okay, bye for now."

I hung up with a smile and a feeling for warmth. I'd needed to end the call about fifteen minutes earlier, but I had enjoyed being a fly on the virtual phone wall. After shooting a quick text of thanks and love you to my mom, I stood up to head back inside.

THE ESSENCE OF TIMELINESS

On the phone call, Ruhi had let us know he was going to be moving back to Hawaii in the next month or sooner, and might not have his government-sponsored cell phone anymore. In fact, we had been able to connect during a strangely well-timed window, as typically he would not have had a cell phone. He had just recently acquired a small tablet he could type emails on—previously, he'd been off grid.

Ruhi was not comfortable in his current living situation, a small apartment. This was due to a tenant upstairs with anger issues, a pit bull, and a baby on the way. He had a caseworker, who arranged a voucher for his flight back to Moloka'i, the old leper island of the Hawaiian chain. In our first few days of corresponding he explained he could potentially be back in Hawaii within a couple of weeks, though the COVID climate of the fall of 2020 gave all of his plans a bit of flex. Therefore, time was of the essence. He emailed me his address and I sent back:

Tue 10/6/2020 10:37 AM

To: Marc Frank <marcruhifrank8@gmail.com>

Thank you, Ruhi, it was great to visit with you and Debra. I would like to hear more about your family, and if you want to talk about your upcoming decision I would enjoy listening. I teach from 7-4 Monday-Friday, if there is a best time to call let me know, or feel free to call anytime. Take care, and thank you for being open, kind, and receptive,

Dylan

Tue 10/6/2020 10:42 AM

To: Moro, Dylan

You're most welcome!

Tue 10/6/2020 2:02 PM

To: Marc Frank <marcruhifrank8@gmail.com>

Hi Ruhi,

I ordered two DNA kits, one from Ancestry.com and one from 23andme. I expedited shipping and they should arrive in the next few days. When the kit arrives, the instructions are fairly straightforward and involve you adding saliva to the tube, attaching some stickers, I believe, and mailing the tube in. I'm not sure on how long results take, I think in the range of a month or so. I can't express how much I humbly appreciate your kindness and willingness to find out our potential genetic connection. It has been truly great visiting with you, and I look forward to keeping in touch. I will follow up with you by phone, and always feel free to call or email me anytime.

All the best,
Dylan

Tue 10/6/2020 3:22 PM

To: Moro, Dylan

Okay, Dylan, shall let you know when it arrives & is sent on. I doubt I will be in this apartment much longer, so the results, are they being sent to you?

Ruhi

WAS IT REAL?

It had been a whopping thirty-six hours, and the adventure had gone from ginger root, to forwarded emails times two, to his email denying he was Ruhi, to his phone call in the same vein of denial, to me convincing both to take a call together, to even more fogginess about her recollection, to Deb asking to potentially certify one way or another with a DNA test, to kits sent to his temporary Florida address, to a nearby future where he might be off grid on the most unpopulated island in Hawaii without internet or cell phone.

But, in this moment, I really felt like I'd found him. I felt certain the DNA would confirm my intuition. Deb had even come around to agreeing his cadence and the soft kindness to his voice seemed familiar to her as well. She had started to connect the facts that he was in the same location during the same period, that he was in essence a wandering poet, that he had two first names, and the pen name Ruhi.

It all seemed to be a lot of coincidence, but, hey, who knows? I knew DNA tests occasionally did not process for various reasons, such as inadequate cells within the saliva, improper collection of samples, tainted samples through shipment, and other issues that could render the specimen unacceptable, such as alcohol or nicotine use.

So I doubled up, with kits from Ancestry and 23andMe. Plus, I thought it would be an interesting way to see who he might connect with on both platforms, including Beverly, Janice, and others. Sending two kits was also a built-in, double-checking mechanism.

Tue 10/6/2020 4:09 PM

> To: Marc Frank <marcruhifrank8@gmail.com>

> Yes, Ruhi, after you submit the vial with your saliva, your results will all populate digitally online and you will have access to see them. If you are indeed my close genetic relative, you will show up as a close contact for me as well. Therefore, you will not need to be in the apartment to receive anything through the mail other than this initial kit that will be sent to you in the next few days. There will be two kits for comparison. Thank you again for being willing. You are very kind.

Tue 10/6/2020 4:19 PM

> To: Moro, Dylan

> Okay, I understand. Phone I have now doesn't work in Hawaii. Shall have to replace it later on. For now, I keep it.

He also shared with me a Blogspot page of his poetry, which a friend had helped him put online.

> Ruki Rumi Marc Frank *http://rukirumi.blogspot.com/*
> with 58 poems listed Posted 23rd October 2013 by Unknown

It opens with the following introduction and includes fifty-eight other original poems:

I have spent my life wandering. It is an interesting and unusual
way of life. It takes courage and abandonment to fate, for it is
a life of freedom. Something deep within me compelled me
to renounce an ordinary life in the world and to take the road
of adventure to experience living in the active present without thought of consequences for the future and survival in the
world. I sought, for one thing, the meaning of existence and the
freedom to experience my own Real Self.

It was a work I promised myself and God to fulfill no matter
what, and to continue expanding myself, no matter the cost. In
the depths of my soul, I determined to experience as much of
life my courage and wits would permit, and I wouldn't com-
promise myself to settle for a mature life, nor stop anywhere
too long lest I become asleep. I would simply gamble all of me

on this quest to experience life fully and innocently before my physical death; and if I could, to write about it.

This was to be my calling, that this journey would take me to the truth of the inner mystical life of a poet's soul—the search for God as a lover born from the vision of beauty and the act of the art of a poet's nature to create from language the essence of inner experiences and the language of love that only a poet's heart can feel and give self expression to as the voice of the divine. That silent voice within was to guide and direct my life through the years of wandering because it gave the divine the experiences of living in the role of a wandering poet.

Looking at his photo, I again saw my physical features in his calves, shoulders and general posture. I thanked him for sharing his poems and intro story. He said a friend had helped him put the webpage together years previously, and it was the only of his works that he knew of being online. He updated me on his potential move. As I would continue to find, it was a fluid situation.

Wed 10/7/2020 12:08 PM

To: Marc Frank <marcruhifrank8@gmail.com>

Hi Ruhi,

When you receive the two kits in the mail over the next few days, they will have activation codes that I will need in order to register them online. If you can write the codes down and email or text them to me, I should be able to set everything up. The Ancestry code is on the tube, and the 23andMe may be on the tube or a card, I'm not certain. Thanks again, we can talk through the process as they arrive. Be well,

Dylan

Wed 10/7/2020 1:04 PM

To: Moro, Dylan

I will, Dylan. Run into a snag with my housing voucher. My caseworker said she has to give the landlord thirty days notice & I have to wait till the end of November & not leave for Hawaii this month. Such is life in this world of people. So I wait.

Ruhi

CHAPTER TWENTY-SIX

NOT ALL RAINBOWS

For two years I had attempted to track this man down, and now, after overcoming what seemed almost impossible chances in connecting, he could roll back into the unknown. The whole situation was making me feel anxious. Ruhi shared with me that he had been diagnosed with Leukemia years previously and had chosen not to receive treatment, as he didn't see it worth the risk versus the reward to go through chemo. He also let me know that he was being treated for a different cancer while in Florida that was requiring surgery.

I didn't press too hard. But he was seventy-five and had some health issues stacked against him. Compound that with him having put his body through some extremes as a wandering traveler throughout his lifetime, and simple math indicated his days may be limited. My proactive inner self desired to seize the moment, and tried to assert some type of control over the situation. I sent the DNA kits his way and hoped that I would have definitiveness for myself.

Regardless of the DNA evidence we got back from the kits, without the actual *Petals of Light* poetry book, Ruhi was still going to have his doubts. He'd made it known to me that the DNA evidence did not matter to him. He was happy to help if the DNA results did matter to me, but he was indifferent to the science behind it. He didn't care, and he didn't care to learn. He felt as if he had lived his life, and he was ready and awaiting his last adventure reuniting with God.

He wasn't being rude in sharing these beliefs, in fact his explanation was kind. But in our conversations, he didn't ask me questions to get to know me on a deeper level, or look for some type of human connection, as one might expect between a potential biological son and father. He corresponded with a friend named Marta, and he would forward me emails that she'd replied back to with his email thread attached at bottom. Whether he meant to do it or not, I couldn't fully tell. But for me, the emails offered possible insights into his train of thought.

Marta would call me a kind lad, and would tell Ruhi this was a chance to connect with a biological son. His original email would say something to the effect of, Dylan is asking me to do a DNA test—I will do as he wishes, though to me, it makes no difference.

It wasn't that I had a void to fill in terms of a male father figure—I was completely satisfied and supported by my dad. And I hadn't expected, if I found Ruhi, for him to want to build a perfect relationship immediately. In fact, I had more been preparing myself for how I might cope or move on if I learned he was not a good man. Perhaps I wasn't fully prepared for how to react to detachment and indifference.

The lyrics from The Lumineers song "Stubborn Love" ran through my mind, "It's better to feel pain, then nothing at all. The opposite of love is indifference." The only thing worse than not following through on love was to be indifferent to it.

That being said, I wasn't hurt. I was just fine. I had a beautiful family. My wife made me a better human, and she supported me with great resilience and toughness. My daughter was simply instant joy. My parents loved me at all times, and were with me on this journey. My siblings and extended friends and family were better humans than me. I was good.

I just selfishly wanted to see this search through. And if that wasn't enough, I felt the urge to meet him in person, even during a pandemic. I didn't think it would change our dynamic. I just didn't want to miss the opportunity to be able to sit next to him on the beach, safely socially distanced, and look him in the eye. I wanted to share a few moments and maybe words, or maybe quiet. Would it be like looking in a physical mirror reflecting the future? Or would it not really matter? I didn't know yet.

BUILDING A RELATIONSHIP

Ruhi had strange rules about how to email back when responding. I felt a small bit of annoyance, as is common for children with parents, but had the self-recognition and awareness to be able to see how silly that was in this situation. Instead I attempted to respect his wishes in what had become a daily correspondence, while taking a crack at what seemed to be his love language. Both were attempts to get on his level and self-involved humor:

Thu 10/8/2020 3:56 AM

>
> Each their own experience
> Each their own mentality
>
> The World turns with or without humans indifferently
>
> Ruki Rumi

Thu 10/8/2020 5:33 AM

To: Marc Frank <marcruhifrank8@gmail.com>

Pursuing purpose through service
To give without expectation
At times impossible
Shuffling through semi-invited white noise
As new life promotes daily direction

A poor attempt.... appreciate info on Hawaii move, all will work out as intended? Thank you for morning verses, and enjoy your morning by the gulf,

Dylan

Thu 10/8/2020 6:17 AM

More actions
To: Moro, Dylan

Good morning, Dylan.

Please don't email me on any poems I may send. Please start a fresh new email.

I try to keep poems as poems under poems.

Thank you,
Ruhi

Thu 10/8/2020 6:57 AM

To: Marc Frank <marcruhifrank8@gmail.com>

Sounds good, Ruhi, will do in the future,

Dylan

COMMUNE-I-CATE

Ruhi had a nontraditional way of communication. At least, different from what had been my normal. I shared a song I had once written in poem form, thinking he may react with some type of insight or guided edit, as poetry seemed to be his love language. But it seemed, in his case, expectations were moot. Simple presentation of information, regardless of an attached response, was best:

MORO, DYLAN
Sat 10/10/2020 2:29 PM

Give me a bike, pedal frustrations below
B/P jumps cross the prairie is where I roll

To the badlands....

There's a native dude with a smile reflecting his beat-up car
I pass two kids strutting, stomping pavement miles from town
Put my head down, eyes stuck to my brow
Clouds go for days, they pop clay peaks somehow

In the badlands, that's where I go

When you are with me here, best storms and stars appear
Brando's backwards cap, rides a light beam above
A rancher man throws me a wave, still looks rough and tough

In the badlands, in the badlands, in the badlands
That's where I go

I wish you would, honey I wish you would get to them badlands
I found good yes, I found good in the badlands
I think we would oh heck I know we would in the badlands

In the badlands....

Sent from my iPhone

MARC FRANK <marcruhifrank8@gmail.com>
Sat 10/10/2020 2:41 PM

Thank you, Dylan, was this one of your experiences?

We had been corresponding with simple pleasantries, some pictures of nature, Zu, poems and writings, and he started to share his life travels in story form. He was always kind when I would write to him, and would say things such as, "thank you for thinking of me, Dylan." One of his hundreds of selections:

Cloudless sky
Sweet waves sounds
Sea salt air fine
Soothing calm
Beauty nature's effect

Ruhi

Sailboats spent time with boats with live aboard sailors some
who sailed
around the world

They were good company

I thought to buy a small
live aboard with my little savings but my body too
old to live like the real hermits sailing around on the oceans of
the Earth

I got to experience that
way of life & a sailor's world is the world they sail around

Like Al & Helen on their Carroll Tahiti Ketch they sailed around
the world four times written up in Guineas world records for the
sailboats size 35 ft & they having lived twenty-five years in that
way of
life

We were sitting on deck
watching sun set
Al says

We never missed a sun rise
We never missed a sun set

Marc & Ruhi

We never

Because of his unfamiliarity with current technology, as was the case with
many of his older peer group, he would occasionally unintententionally
forward me emails that provided insight as to what he might have been
thinking, even as his words were indifferent.

In one such email, he had forwarded my picture on to Marta, his close lifelong friend. Marta was a friend to the Dalai Lama when she lived in North India, and in Calcutta she worked with Mother Theresa and wrote a book on her experience published in French in Paris, France.

He included me on an email he forwarded of my picture, with a caption reading, "This is Dylan, who thinks I may be his biological father." He followed up quickly with: "Sorry, Dylan, machine automatically sent to you, was intending it for a friend to share." The image he had shared.

Ruhi's friend Marta seemed to be a kind and positive voice of reason:

MARC FRANK <marcruhifrank8@gmail.com>
Sun 10/11/2020 10:17 AM

To: Moro, Dylan

A friend Marta in Poland said to say hi to you. She commented
that your eyes are like my eyes.

I needed to accept a patient role, but this was not fully in my nature. As I waited for the kits to arrive, I felt an urge to find out more. It was an odd feeling to have found a connection, but not yet being privy to the full extent of information I had assumed would be available. As I started to get more of a sense of Marc's comfort level, I found it easier to accept his personality and wishes as they were.

I think what helped was my childhood of having been exposed to many unique characters and personalities via my parents' social network. I could keep an easy-going approach, even if the real Ruhi didn't perfectly fit into the "Ruhi" box I had mentally created. I was, in a sense, predisposed to accept unorthodox characters. Or perhaps it was simply my chromosomes that allowed for an ease of adaptation. Like, even if I didn't fully get it, my genes did.

Ruhi was kind and willing to talk about subjects that seemed most important to him, such as spiritual connections, stories of travels through India, and others he had met along the way. He had a genuine authenticity that was quirky, and didn't seem to be hiding anything.

LEARNING ABOUT
HIS WORLD AND WHAT IF

I took his phone call over the car speaker coming back from our tree house yurt up in the Black Hills. Zu was car-seated in the back. Marc had opened up freely about his travels and experiences. It was early within our correspondence, and I was wishing I had a notepad and the ability to write down each word as it came out. I had a feeling of having fleeting time with him, stemming from the challenge and rarity of the find, his potential cancer, and his move to who knows where and when. It felt like just as easily as he had appeared that morning after I randomly stumbled upon the ginger article, he could disappear.

Ruhi spoke of his travels to India, living in various communities from coast to coast, walking the Southwest desert, watching the sun set in the Southeast and growing up with a military father who had served through three wars, WWII, Korean, and Nam. He shared about his mother, who he said was a sweet, beautiful woman whose family had come through Ellis Island. His father, he said, told him at a young age, in an unloving fashion and a cold, matter-of-fact way, "I never took to you, Marc."

I mostly listened through the hour-long conversation, but I had one, ever-important query for Ruhi. Did he know of any other potential children? If I was out here, in what seemed like such a random pathway of creation, and if his biggest stated regret was not being celibate throughout life, then a betting man might venture to think there could be others.

The others would technically be my half siblings, and we would unknowingly share half of the genetic blueprint that would determine our phenotype from genotype. Finding siblings could be another interesting adventure—perhaps the most interesting adventure of the entire journey. Ruhi spoke of a boy named Adam, and an old friend of his, Johnny S., who may have helped to raise a young girl.

THE JOURNAL AND PERSPECTIVE

The first sixth-grade student I met to start the once-in-a-lifetime 2020 pandemic school year was Lenny. He was a happy, spirited boy who was kind and sharp right off the bat. All the other students were left out of the school until the actual first day, as the world attempted to navigate the unknown repercussions of bringing students back into a closed building setting with or without required masks, with or without distant or hybrid learning, and with or without a vaccine or "herd immunity."

Lenny came into the building solo to tour his new setup, under the steady watch of a behavior specialist teacher. This teacher would be Lenny's best advocate and resource throughout what was being projected as challenging year for him—not because of the pandemic, but because it was going to be his first year of stability in his twelve years of living. Lenny had been in and out of foster homes, but now had settled in with a social worker who was set to adopt him and provide some much-needed stability. Lenny smiled at me and, as if he'd known me for years, presented me with a handmade journal he had worked on.

Its cover was a thick cardboard, with a map design on the back and front. Inside, he had self-cut fifty or so pages out of regular eight-by-ten white printer paper. Two gold rings held the binding together, and the best touch was the leather tie that Lenny showed me how to use to open and close the journal. I was immediately humbled. Here was a young person who had already had a substantially harder life than the one I'd been privileged to live, and he was giving selflessly and without any expectations.

I immediately went into unrehearsed and off-the-cuff flattery. It was my bread-and-butter move, and it complemented, if nothing else, my unique social skill set. I had been deploying this skill for as long as I can remember. I was able to present myself as both humble and as a sponge, eager to learn, and I could make others and myself feel good about it. I employed these skills in a variety of situations, whether it was complimenting older dudes on the ball court when I was a skinny eight-year-old trying to get in the ball game; or stepping into the varsity coxswain role with a boat full of experienced senior studs with great leadership, having just come off the best OSU varsity finish in the history of the program, just outside of the medals at fourth place.

I was mostly authentic and genuine in my approach, especially when I was legitimately humbled, informed, improved, or had some angle to gain. I was born with enough innate intellect to understand that I have a manipulative quality I needed to keep in check, but I often failed at doing so. In other words, this was a self-serving characteristic—I could present myself in whatever way was needed in most situations, for my personal gain. When Lenny passed me this gift that he had put some reasonable time into, especially as a twelve-year-old, it brought out true appreciation and humility from me.

I told him, "Dude, this is awesome, I am going to have special things to put into this notebook. I'm not entirely sure what they'll be yet, but I will keep you posted and I will put this to good use."

Months later, when I shared with Lenny that the journal had become my home base as I took notes on my journey to track down my biological father, the sparkle in his eye told me he was using my own tact against me—or maybe more so with me. He said, "Cool."

As I briefly shared where I was in the process of finding my biological father, I felt a sharp slap of reality, as I had many times over the past years and, really, my lifetime. I could see the perspective of what my life of privilege meant, especially when compared to the situations of others. I'm not sure if most people compare themselves to others in this way, but for me comparison has always been an Achilles' heel. It's a bit competitive, a bit judgmental, and a bit ridiculous. At the end of the day, it has little benefit, and it's something within me that I have needed to work on to curb.

Lenny's story is one of not having a consistent parental figure, male or female, for the entirety of his life. In giving me this journal, without ever having met me, and just as he was embarking on his own new journey with potential for stability, he made me take score of what I truly had.

I had parents who loved me unconditionally. I had siblings, both on my side and Keen's, who not only put up with my BS but who actually liked and believed in me. I had friends who took my relentless teasing, which I called playful tough love, and still cared about me. I had a wife who kept me balanced, challenged me, loved me, and provided for me. I married into a family that did all of the above. I had a daughter who, every morning when I wake up and hear her little voice and start the day with eye-to-eye contact, provides unrelenting purpose to my heart beating and my lungs taking in oxygen. I had former players I had coached, teammates, and co-workers who had humored me as they dealt with me throughout my life, and who had been steadfast in their respect for me and who mentored me into becoming a better version of myself.

And now I had a new biological story. I had another being to help me to look analytically in the mirror and to search my mind to relearn who I was. Potentially, I could also have other humans out there made up of the same stuff as me, who I could potentially form relationships with.

As I opened the leather shoelace-tied binding, I started scribbling in my terrible, all-caps handwriting, modeled after Johnny's and made worse by years of longhand nursing notes. I was writing with the intention of someday giving this journal to Zu:

<u>Finding Ruhi</u>

1. Evie's birth 2018, DNA results came back ½ Ashkenazi Jewish?

2. Jer did 23andMe, ½ sister.

3. Uncle Jimmy (John Dad's) bro did not show up on Ancestry.

4. Cousins Aaron, John Carl, Mindy all accurately first cousins—none Jewish.

5. Janice W. closest Jewish relative, non-responsive when contacted.

Page 2:

1. Beverly C. later showed up as same % relation as first cousins. I placed as bio-father's half-sister.

2. Talked with my mom, she spoke of a traveling poet who went by "Ruhi" & "Looked like old paintings of Jesus"

3. No last or first names, possibly two first-type names.

4. 4. One poetry book, *Petals of Light* he had written & given.

Page 3:

1. Google searches for next two yrs—empty.

2. Some online poetry written by a "Ruhi" from 2016, but no response, seemed like a ghost.

3. Followed up w/ Beverly's granddaughter JeTaunne L. for any info, but closed adoption.

4.   Mom thought perhaps Portland contact/spiritual group of "Preemies" might know, but no memory.

Page 4:

1.   Sept 2020 Googled "Ruhi Cornell Poet" after distant Canadian relative Yifaht K. said she had a Cornell professor relative.

2.   Found a 2012 article about a "biker dude" Hugh J.'s ginger root farm on the Big Island Hawaii.

3.   Emailed his wife, who forwarded on to Hugh and then Ruhi.

Page 5:

1.   Got an early a.m. email, then call, from Ruhi, stating he didn't think he was the "Ruhi" I was looking for, as did not remember Debra.

2.   Had three-way call with my mom & him, she thought she recognized the kind, gentle cadence in his voice.

3.   Emailed Ruhi relatives of Janice W.'s mother obit. He recognized names Elkin & Bush from his mother's side.

Page 6:

1.   Asked Ruhi to do a DNA test, he said he would if I wished and also wanted to know truth.

2.   Oct 23rd, 2020, early morn results back & confirmed he was bio-father.

3. Keen, John, Deb, all fam supportive & Ruhi Marc Frank
    also kind.

On the next page I stuck a bright neon yellow Post-It note with a note written in blue permanent pen: 10/23/20: "I found him, Mark "Ruhi" Frank. 23andMe DNA results back this morn. We checked together in early sunny a.m. You (Zu), Mom & me = +

Even as I felt confident in the genetic connection, I still had a hint of disconnect with the idea of him being my biological father. For me, the importance of connecting with Ruhi was more physical than mental, emotional, or spiritual. I felt more of those non-physical connections my dad, Johnny, who had nurtured me day after day and whose values I carried within. It wasn't a competition, but my attraction to Ruhi at first was more in the interest of a family story I could share with Zu down the road. It was typical me, and of course I was attempting to jump the gun:

Fri 10/9/2020 9:30 AM

To: Marc Frank <marcruhifrank8@gmail.com>

Good morning, Ruhi,

I hope you are doing well today. If you have time or the willingness, would you be able to email me family names (first and
last) of your parents, grandparents, siblings, cousins, uncles/
aunts, children (Aaron from Washington (or his mother),
didn't catch the last name), and the Ukranian women, child,
and man that helped to raise. Any other family historical
information would be of great interest. You mentioned parents
or grandparents traveling through Ellis Island and changing
their last name to Frank, Holocaust survival, time in Paris and
your travels through India and beyond. I would be very interested in any historical information you would feel comfortable

and want to share. We can talk on the phone as well, but with written names it helps me to piece information together. If not, no worries, and I understand. Take care,

Dylan

Fri 10/9/2020 9:59 AM

To: Moro, Dylan

Sorry, Dylan, you're asking too much. It takes too much time & energy. Ruhi

Fri 10/9/2020 10:38 AM

To: Marc Frank <marcruhifrank8@gmail.com>

No problem, Ruhi, thank you for your honesty. Dylan

To: Moro, Dylan

You're welcome, have good day.

I was still locked into an investigative role as well. It was a hard hat to remove after two years of nightly time put in.

CHAPTER TWENTY-SEVEN

SCIENTIFIC EVIDENCE

After Ruhi received the kit, he spit in the tube and put it back in the mail without sending me the correct code on the label to register the kit. I was able to call 23andMe and straighten out his sample and set up a profile.

I received updates after Ruhi's saliva sample was sent away:

23andme.com@mg.23andme.com on behalf of **23andMe**

Sat 10/17/2020 10:01 AM

To: Moro, Dylan

Mark "Ruhi",

Your sample is at our lab and in queue for DNA extraction. This step usually takes 1-2 weeks. Your results are expected by November 7. We've received the saliva sample registered to:

Mark "Ruhi" Frank

We will soon start the process of separating your DNA from your saliva.

Sincerely,
The 23andMe Team

Sun 10/18/2020 10:33 PM

To: Moro, Dylan

Mark "Ruhi", we're genotyping your DNA

This step usually takes 3-10 days.

Your results are expected by November 7.

On to genotyping! Thanks to this technology, we're able to read around 600,000 letters in your DNA, which power your 23andMe results. We use probes to turn your sample into knowledge.

Sincerely,
The 23andMe Team

Wed 10/21/2020 5:00 PM

To: Moro, Dylan

Mark "Ruhi", we're reviewing your genetic data

This step usually takes 1-3 days. Your results are expected by November 7.

Using powerful computers and software, scientists on our analysis team have received your raw data from the lab and are making sense of it. During analysis, colors are translated into your DNA letters, and important quality control happens. This is the final step before your results are ready.

Sincerely,
The 23andMe Team

Fri 10/23/2020 9:29 AM

Mark "Ruhi",
Welcome to you!

The 23andMe results for Mark "Ruhi" Frank are in.

A world of DNA discovery is waiting.

It was the 23rd of October, 2020, just shy of three weeks after I had found
the ginger root article, and the science had come to call. As my gut, mind,
layman's investigative work, and Mom's intuition had indicated, this was
"the Ruhi." The needle in the haystack, the single grain in the plains, the
lone star in the cosmos, the wandering poet amongst the 8 million with
only a pen name was, in fact, my genetic father, and I had found him with
the help of many.

> ***23andMe's results from Ruhi's Dashboard:***
> **Your genetic relationship to John Dylan Moro**
> Relationship
> Son
>
> *Hide DNA details*
>
> Shared DNA
> 47.5%
> 3531cM
>
> ***23andMe's results from my Dashboard:***
> **Your genetic relationship to Marc "Ruhi" Frank**
> Relationship
> Father
>
> *Hide DNA details*

Shared DNA

47.5%

3531cM

EYE TO EYE POTENTIAL

So what next? While I had been waiting for these pending results, I had already set my mind on what my heart felt—I needed to be with him in person. The timeframe didn't matter so much, but I felt if I never had the opportunity to share a physical presence to connect, something would be left unfulfilled.

I navigated the logistics, using a delicate touch, with the people who mattered most in terms of a potential visit: Keen and Zu, my parents, my work, and Ruhi (which I was continuing to call him, as it seemed appropriate and still fit). We were deep into a once-a-generation pandemic, something the world hadn't seen since the Spanish Flu, but I had a minimalist tendency when it needed to be engaged. Through my upbringing, traveling through Africa, and nursing school, I had honed the skills of needing very little and of living with the essentials.

I convinced Keen that I could camp out along the way, with a few shower stops at her siblings' homes in Iowa and Indiana. I would pack a cooler and only stop to gas up, take a whiz on the side of the road, and hit drive-throughs only if food was needed. It would be a contactless journey, as the last thing that I wanted was to contract COVID and expose Ruhi in the process.

The window of opportunity pointed to the upcoming Thanksgiving break, as I could take two personal days and turn it into a full week, plus weekends. That way I'd have the ability to drive versus flying, which brought the inevitable potential for increased exposure. It would also allow for long talks, and time to process and think about the gravity of my singular focus and effort over the past two years.

Keen was supportive. She said she thought I should go, and that if I didn't I would regret it. She was aware of Ruhi's current situation. She knew time could be of the essence, given how finicky his consistent living situation appeared, not to mention his age and that he was being actively treated for cancer and had indicated that he had untreated Leukemia. The poems he had been sharing with me daily seemed to indicate that he was not only ready to meet his reunion with the divine, but he was welcoming it.

My principal was supportive as well, so long as I could find a willing sub during the pandemic, which I was able to do. Johnny and Deb not only understood the trip, but made sure I knew if the logistics and timing were different, they would perhaps want to go as well, and they looked forward to the day when they too might be able to meet Ruhi.

The last domino in what seemed like the culmination of my journey would prove to be the most challenging. Ruhi had made clear on previous phone calls that he was indifferent to our relationship being confirmed by a DNA test. Really, he seemed indifferent to the whole idea of learning of a potential biological son. It did not matter to him, and he was not expressing this out of cruelty, but out of honesty. In his mind, he had lived his life and he was on the last phase of his journey. It did not make a difference to him what role I may or may not have in it. While his words could be taken as harsh, his actions and gentle kindness were enough for me and helped me not get too caught up in the details of his words. After all, he had been in denial of our biologic connection since the first morning email and call, and that was okay—I never had expectations for him, I had set out only to give Ruhi the opportunity to learn of the truth and do what he would like with the information.

Besides, the journey wasn't all about him. Selfishly, I had my own desires. I wanted to be able to tell Zu in a tangible, honest, and authentic way about her genealogical history. Plus, I wanted to finish my quest. The other boxes had been checked, so the in-person visit was now mostly for myself.

In complete honesty, there was also a part of me that thought, hey, he's human. If he sees me in person, he too may feel a connection, regardless of the indifference he claims over the phone. This was a slight nod to Luke and Vader. Luke could still feel the human good within his father regardless of how dark Vader had become. Yes, Ruhi was my Vader, only nothing like him at all.

I caught Ruhi a bit caught off guard when I proposed coming to visit. When he returned my missed call and I posed the potential visit, I was sitting on a downed cottonwood trunk next to Spearfish Creek with Zu on my lap. A few days earlier, I had shared that his DNA results came back and he was my biological father. I offered to screenshot the results for him so he could see for himself, and he reiterated his indifference. Again, he said it didn't matter, that he was fine to help if it was my wish, but it made no difference for him. The poem book *Petals of Light* would be his legitimate proof. Science, he felt, was skewed and had too many possibilities for inaccuracy.

Here I could feel a stark division and diversion in our natural congruence. Science was my fact. The poem book would be interesting, sure, but it held no certainty for me. He and my mom both were hazy on their separate and combined recollection of nearly forty years in the past. But one thing Ruhi afforded me, intentionally or not, was the opportunity to self-reflect. Maybe I was wrong. Random lab techs taking saliva samples and pairing them might not hold as much weight as a book of poetry he produced in his own writing, which had laid dormant all these years awaiting the reopening to connect and certify. Perhaps this was the reason my mom hadn't dumped the book off earlier, keeping it through multiple family moves. Or, wait—she couldn't find it. She finally admitted she'd probably had pitched it during one of our family moves, though she couldn't recall for certain.

Either way, the science had spoken. Of the nearly 8 billion peeps wandering around, I had sent a sample, and puppeteered Ruhi sending a sample, to an unknown lab run by strangers, and the results had spoken clearly. I was made up of half of the stuff that he was. Period. So as he hesitated at the thought of me visiting, I changed my tactics a bit. Instead of a careful, patient approach, my true self came out. I pushed back.

"Listen, Ruhi, I don't have any expectations of you, I just want to have a moment in person to spend some time in each other's company. We can sit on the beach outside at a safe distance."

He said he would pray on it that night and let me know how he felt, but my hunch was that he would not be willing at this point in time. I worried this was a tangible window that might close. Zu was going to be fine if I was gone for a week, as would Keena, who had days off coming up and my mother-in-law Karen available to help out. Ruhi was still out there, alive, and I knew where he was located at this moment and could drive directly to him.

My hypothetical prognostication was that, given a few weeks or months, he could be disconnected from technological communication. He could be living in a completely different place. Or, as he seemed to desire, he could be done with this life in the flesh. My opportunity was now, and I wanted to strike while the iron was hot. I wanted to see this journey through to an in-person recognition of biological connection, genetic father and son, right or wrong.

CHAPTER TWENTY-EIGHT

COULD THERE BE MORE? COINCIDENTAL DYLAN

I had attempted to pump the brakes on committing to following up on potential siblings until there was genetic verification. I didn't want to create any strange uncertainty with others I would need to contact, including potential half siblings. But upon receiving Ruhi's DNA results, I was all in.

In talking with Ruhi, he had mentioned one particular woman he had been close to, a Polish refugee who had raised her child with a mutual friend. Johnny S., the friend, became a significant part of the girl's life when she was little, and provided some support when Ruhi traveled on. Johnny S., Ruhi told me, had spent his life's work giving an outlet to Oregon prisoners through a successful Shakespeare theater program. A simple Google search gave me a contact from his new venture website. I submitted an initial reach-out email, updating this Johnny on my current situation, outlining who I was, my connection to Marc/Ruhi, and my interest in tracking down any other potential family.

Johnny S. called me back the next day. He was jovial and kind on the phone, and conversation was easy. While filling me in on his relationship with Marc, he gave me some great backstory on who Marc had been when they'd known each other. He told a story of Marc having met Bob Dylan, my coincidental namesake, that cemented my impression that Marc was a genuine person who was quite literal in his approach to life. The story goes that someone told Marc he should meet Bob Dylan, and he said, "okay," and went to the musician's house and slept on his porch. The next morning, he was invited inside, where Dylan shared his life story. Ruhi said, "okay," and traveled on.

Coincidentally, Ruhi later shared an email explaining the encounter from his own perspective:

MARC FRANK <marcruhifrank8@gmail.com>
Mon 11/16/2020 9:40 PM

Another night of sleeplessness, so I write, and listen to Bob Dylan, a very good songwriter of my generation. We met in the sixties in Greenwich Village on Manhattan Island.

I had come back from India.
It was wintertime in New York. Had an awful time of it being homeless in the cold snowy weather. Didn't have warm clothes or much money, like usual. Yet I didn't
care as long as my heart & head was on God.

Would hang out in the coffee shops to keep warm, where there were poets, folk singers, painters, etc. Someone was always performing with the hat for donations. Read poems a couple of times, and it got me a flower, a few dollars, free coffee & a meal, but I didn't take to it. Didn't like standing in front of audiences, though I did it different times in different places, includ-ing a radio interview at Evergreen State College in Olympia, Washington State & at Berkeley California & North Beach San Francisco.

Met known poets & unknown poets & it was all the process of learning & experiencing life.

At night I'd walk through Washington Square Park to NYU
student union & rest in one of the cushioned chairs & be out of
the cold.

Tough life, looking back, but my body was young & I could
take hardships & distress.

So I was in a cafe, a man was
playing the piano. He bought
me a cup of coffee & began talking. He invites me to a party,
telling me

Bob Dylan will be there. Meet me here tonight. We'll walk over.

At that time I didn't know who
Bob Dylan was. I was out of
the country so much wandering the world. I can't even claim I
was part of the sixties movements. I was quite on the outside, as
I always been very detached.

In the cafe he tells me the
party is called off, yet he says

You should meet Bob, here's
his address.

He writes it down & we part. I walk to the student union at NYU
to rest & keep warm.

While sitting there writing,
the clerk at the candy counter came up to me with a bag of can-
dies he offers to me, saying

Whenever you come in I feel
at peace. I want you to have this.

At different times I heard people say they felt peace around me,
though I suffered.

Those paradoxes of life.

Next day I walked over to McDougal Street to Bob Dylan's
address, coming out
from the brownstone house
a young man around my age
with a boy child on his shoulders.

Are you Bob Dylan? I asked, I
was told to meet you.

He took a couple of steps back, looked me over. He said

I can't talk now I have somewhere to go.

He walked off with the child
on his shoulders & I passed the day keeping warm.

Life is very simple when you know your needs, not so much
your wants. My body needed warmth, that's all I had to do &
remember God
& write!

Evening came on. I felt prompted to walk back to Bob's house. It
was cold & I
saw through the glass door
a radiator in the small foyer
& a glass door in the inside
& the outside door to the sidewalk, I tried the door knob it
turned & I went inside, feeling the warmness from the radiator.

Sat down on the floor, leaning my back on the wall. Soon I was
lying down on the floor, very tired & rested. The foyer
was big enough to fold up my
legs & lie on my side.

I was resting. I heard a door
open & then the inside door
to the foyer open. There was
the same young man I met earlier outside the door.

I recall he reached down with his arm stretched out to help
me up.

I said, it's alright, I can get up
on my own.

Got up on my feet than he began talking

I am sorry for the way I behaved toward you before.
I have strangers coming up to me wanting to talk. I have a
man looking through my trash can. It wasn't what I set out to do.

He was breaking down crying.

All I wanted was to write my songs & sing. This fame is
killing me. I neglect my family.

He finished. He was quiet as we stood together in the small foiler
with the warmth of the radiator.

I say, I have something for you.

I had the cycle of poems I wrote beginning in Israel & ending in
India that I wrote
in different countries traveling overland. It was in

a black notebook. I wrote it
by hand. In the different countries there were old-fashioned
typewriters, for a few coins the owner provided thick paper &
the typewriter
that was on the street with a small wooden table & a chair or
short stool to sit & type out the poems while the world went by.
Some of the poems
I lost in my travels. Doesn't matter!

I handed him the book. He took it, pressed it to his heart.
He reached out toward me
with the book, saying

I'm afraid I might lose it!

I respond saying

If you lose it, it is lost!

He asks me to come back in three days. I go out into the cold
dark night. As I walked through Washington Square Park, it was
snowing on my way to the student union at NYU.

I said outlook

Lord, if ever I am to be known
as a poet please let it be when I am mature enough to handle it.

Time passes, I run into a man I used to know out in Oregon. He
buys me lunch. We eat together & talk. He works on the New
York Times newspaper. In exchange for a one-way bus ticket to
San Francisco, I give him the book of poems.

He says, I will hold the book for you & writes down his address
& gives me the money for the bus ticket.

I walk uptown to the Port Authority Bus Terminal & wait there
for the next bus with ticket bought.

Three days later, I go back.
His wife invites me into their home, introduces their two
young sons.

She tells me that Bob had to
leave town suddenly & he wanted me to be sure to return your
book. She walked
over to the piano where it sat, handed it to me, saying

Bob said to thank you!

Ruhi / Marc

A little more to this story. I was in an Italian cafe in North
Beach after I arrived by bus to San Francisco, a similar scene to
Greenwich Village.

A man comes up to me. He says

Do you know Bob Dylan has gone to Israel?

That's all he said. Later, walking to Fisherman's Wharf along San
Francisco Bay, had this thought that Bob & I meeting was the
beginning of his spiritual search & his cultural roots as a Jew.

I asked Johnny S. if he thought Ruhi fabricated the truth at all, and he
said, "No, he had no reason to."

Johnny S. said Ruhi was one of the most kindhearted and unadulterated humans he had known. I then asked Johnny S. what I was most
interested in learning more about—the potential of a half sibling. This half
sister might be connected through a woman named Yolanda W., the Polish
refugee he and Ruhi had both known earlier in life. Johnny S. confirmed

that Yolonda and Ruhi had a relationship, and that a child had come from it, a girl named Irene.

I asked if Johnny S. could provide any time frames or geographical references. It was challenging to pin down exact times, he said, but he shared that Irene had been born in Portland, the same city of my birth, and estimated she may have been born very close to the ballpark timeline of my own origin story. Johnny S. had helped support Yolanda with Irene early in her childhood, and then had fallen out of touch with them. Yolanda eventually remarried and relocated to Wisconsin, he thought, and then potentially on to Atlanta. Thinking about the potential for another genetic relative I may share similarities with gave me a familiar, warm sense of connection. In a strange sense, she may be the only other person in the world with a similar frame of reference in terms of an unknown biological father, in this case, potentially the same bio-father.

I also asked this Johnny if he knew anything of an Aaron, who Ruhi had mentioned on the phone previously, a young boy from Washington state who had taken his own life in his early twenties. Johnny did not know anything about Aaron. Shortly after our phone call, he emailed me a link to an NPR audio clip of both Yolanda and Irene from April of 2016:

STORYCORPS

StoryCorps Atlanta: 'I Became The Mother That I Never Had'
MELISSA TERRY • *APR 26, 2016*

JOLANTA HOPKINS AND HER DAUGHTER, IRENE WAZGOWSKA, INTERVIEWED EACH OTHER IN THE STORYCORPS ATLANTA BOOTH.

CREDIT STORYCORPS ATLANTA
4:19 | Play story My List
Listen

> **4:19**
> Jolanta Hopkins was born in Poland to self-proclaimed "un-fit parents." Despite contracting polio at the age of four, however, she had a warm and happy childhood in the home of her paternal grandparents.

Hopkins's absentee mother passed away in Poland late in 2015 whereupon she and her daughter, Irene Wazgowska, made the trip for the funeral.

Hopkins and Wazgowska visited the StoryCorps Atlanta booth shortly after their return as an opportunity to process their feelings and move toward closure.

This story was recorded in partnership with the Atlanta History Center, which hosts Atlanta's StoryCorps Booth.

Above the play button for the audio was an image of two beautiful women with strong jawlines and warm eyes. I had Yolanda's name completely misspelled—Jolanta was correct. I immediately searched for physical similarities, both between mother and daughter and then between the daughter and myself. This search was a strange practice that I was becoming more familiar with after never having done it in the first thirty-five years of my life.

Driving from school to pick up Zu from daycare, I clicked the four-plus-minute audio and sat back. I became fixated on both their tones and the subject matter. It was an awesome moment—I felt connected. Whether it was the product of self-genesis or an authentic, unexplainable atomic directive, Irene seemed familiar.

That night, I set out to find a way to contact her. I found a few postings of some writings she had done in her previous career, along with multiple hits on Rio Energy Bar, a new product she and her partner had been crafting and promoting. From their webpage, I filled out another contact form—I was becoming a seasoned vet at manipulating general contact pages into personal questions about potential connections, using them as a pathway to connect for an entirely different purpose. I kept it simple on the form, not wanting to appear too creepy. Once Irene responded back, I followed up with a more in-depth response, and included a photo since

I felt strange that I knew what she looked like from the NPR story and wanted to reciprocate:

on RIO ENERGY BAR Message Details: Name: **J DYLAN MORO** Email: dylan.moro@k12.sd.us

> Subject: Possible contact with Irene?

> Message: Hello, my name is Dylan Moro, I was hoping to have a chance to correspond with Irene. My cell is 541-908-3039, feel free to reach out at a time that works for you. Thanks very much, and excellent idea with the nutritious bar. Take care,

> Moro, Dylan

Mon 10/26/2020 11:35 AM

RIO ENERGY BAR <4ab9b314-1242-4d3d-a4e8-f89be86e59d9@crm. wix.com>

Mon 10/26/2020 11:11 AM

> You've got a new message

> Hi Dylan, Thanks for reaching out! How can we help you?

> Kindly, Irene

On *Fri, Oct 23, 2020, 7:13 PM* **J DYLAN MORO** <no-reply+231095952962@ crm.wix.com> wrote:

Hi Irene,

Apologies for contacting you in a roundabout way through your business venture (which seems very cool and purposeful). I have been searching for my biological father for the past two years after a DNA test came back showing I was half Jewish (and I was raised by a German/Dutch mother and Italian/Mexican father). My only clues from my mother were that he was a wandering poet who did some spiritual studying with her in Portland, Oregon, 1982 and went by the name "Ruhi."

It's been a true needle-in-the-haystack journey. After many different searches, I tracked down a ginger root farmer on the Big Island, Hawaii, who named a root strain after a poet buddy who went by "Ruhi," and was able to be put in contact with him. Anyway, last weekend I confirmed this man, Marc "Ruhi" Frank, as being my biological father through a DNA test. I have been corresponding with him a bit. He spoke of a potential daughter that I believe, perhaps, might be you?

He also spoke of a potential son who took his own life in his early twenties in Washington state. My wish is not to overwhelm or stress you in any way, so I completely understand if you are not interested in corresponding and will respect your wishes. For me, it has been an interesting journey into my genetics, and the thought of potentially having other half siblings is very intriguing in a positive way.

I am the oldest of four and grew up with three amazing siblings in Oregon, who I now realize are genetically half siblings, and all have been very supportive in this exploration process. I now live in the Black Hills of South Dakota in an outdoorsy little town called Spearfish, my wife Keena is from the Badlands of South Dakota (Kadoka) and we had our first daughter Zuzu in June of 2019 (she's a walking cruiser of exploration now). Anyway, I could be totally off base, but at least wanted to reach out. I'll send you a picture as well, take care and all the best,

Dylan

Again, my cell is 541 908 3039. I am a teacher, but have some preps throughout the day, or evenings are good too.

The next day, I was heading to get our biweekly veggie pickup from a local farm. I pulled over to take a call before I hit the dead cell spot up Higgins Gulch outside of Spearfish. It was Irene. She and her husband Hoomi were

both on the call and I, as I often do, was taking seventy-five percent minimum of the conversation pie. She was very receptive, interjecting short statements and questions as I pre-claused everything with "long story short," which always was followed, ironically, with a long story.

She shared about her life growing up in Wisconsin with two stepsisters and we both paused for short reflection when we realized that her birthdate was only four months before mine. She was a fall of '82 baby and I was born in a February '83. Not only was it crazy cool to think I might technically have an older sibling, but we were potentially genetically related peers.

I asked if she had known about Ruhi, and if she was ever curious about connecting with him. She told me that previously, maybe ten years or so, in her twenties, she had attempted to track him down for medical history purposes. She had his full name and that he lived in Hawaii, but was unable to find him. It was hard not to compare the gravity and chance randomness of my luck in success of finding him years later without a name or location. Truly, what were the odds?

I told her I was thinking of visiting Ruhi in person and would keep her posted. We shared about our families. Keen and I with Zu. Irene and H, as she called him, were expecting their first daughter, who they were planning to name Tulip. My nurtured sentimental nostalgia—from my mom—was dripping as I attempted to draw a connection between Tulip's obvious flower reference and Zuzu's petals, a flower reference from Zu's namesake movie *It's a Wonderful Life*.

Irene and H were both kind to humor my ridiculousness. We ended the call with pleasantries and made plans to stay in contact. It was just a very cool and unique feeling to have connected with Irene and her husband. We both agreed that perhaps there was no such thing as a perfectly nuclear family. Every family seemed to have layers and wrinkles.

My two-year journey was presenting more and more truths and positive connections. It also opened the doorway to envisioning different scenarios, such as what if it hadn't been Ruhi's genetics that had created me in the first place, but always and only my dad Johnny's? This would have given me a different story, one that was arguably easier and more reasonable. Might I have looked a bit different, stood taller, had a different palate, maybe different talents or skills? Or maybe not, maybe I was who I was.

Either way, I definitely would not have made connection with Irene. I wouldn't have shared that phone call and subsequent Zoom and WhatsApp video calls, and would never have felt support and, strangely, a sense of belonging and love from a complete stranger. I also felt a sense of mutual desire from Irene to develop a relationship. Could this simple connection be enough to rationalize the entire journey? Perhaps.

CHAPTER TWENTY-NINE

RUHI'S FAMILY HISTORY

Some family history that I pieced together in talking with Ruhi was that the family name, Frank, had been shortened in coming through Ellis Island around 1910-ish. His father, Floyd Frank, a soldier through three wars, had a disconnected relationship with Ruhi. Marc told a story of when he was a young boy in Paris and his father gave him a scooter, but before Marc could have it or use it, Floyd took the scooter apart and left it up to Marc to piece it back together.

His mother was Florence (Bush) Frank. In describing how his maternal grandmother journeyed to the United States, Ruhi said, "It was the Bolshevik Revolution in Russia, and my mother's mother had to escape the Ukraine."

Ruhi followed the Indian spiritual master Meher Baba throughout life, living in varying communes. He traveled through India for multiple years. He had lived on the Big Island and Molokai in Hawaii.

His sister Sandra lived in upstate New York. He maintained a relationship with Sandra because he promised his parents that he would throughout life. Ruhi encouraged me to call his sister, as she would be more willing and able to share family history information. He made clear that, for him, his family history did not matter, and he was unequipped to handle the energy and knowledge demanded.

I called Sandra. She was very pleasant and a busy talker. She told me they were a military family, and had moved to Germany around 1942. Her mother Florence had said she would not have a child in Oklahoma when stationed there, so Sandra was born in Pittsburgh, Pennsylvania, when the family was back from war. Sandra was born January 4, 1945. Marc was a couple years younger. She said the family essentially had nothing except a Studebaker and a cocker spaniel.

During Marc's childhood, they were stationed in France. She said she and Marc constantly fought as kids. She was introverted as a child and now extroverted, and Marc was the opposite. She said Floyd and Florence were both raised in religious Jewish (Kosher) families. Floyd's siblings had passed, except one brother Marvin in Austin, Texas. There was Vera, Rela, Audrey, Marvin, and Clancey, who had passed at a young age. Florence had one younger brother, Sam.

Florence's mother had passed at twenty-eight years of age. Florence's side of the family were well-off Russians who had moved to the states and sold oranges from a push cart. Floyd had been a proud great-grandfather when he passed in 2014, and Marc had moved to Florida to help care for him toward the end of his life. Florence had lived from 1922-2000 and was a proud great-grandmother. Floyd and Florence were now buried together at a Florida national cemetery. Sandra disclosed that she had felt close to their dad and Marc to their mom.

Sandra had taught English later in life in Korea, and was a GS4-rated civil servant in Vietnam in 1967 working at a Mobile Army Surgical Hospital. She had one daughter, Nadine. She said Marc started traveling at a young age, heading to Mexico instead of signing with foreign military in France. The family later received letters that he had a required physical in D.C. He traveled to India to pursue poetry and a spiritual pathway. She said Marc has had cancer for a long time and that he was currently being treated for skin cancer.

Sandra gave me her address and asked if I would send some pictures, and we thanked each other for the time on the phone. A few months later, I sent her a Christmas picture card.

CHAPTER THIRTY

ON THE ROAD TO COMPLETE THE JOURNEY

I was on the road to Venice, Florida, to meet my biological father Marc "Ruhi" Frank in person. As I cruised down South, it felt like a retreat of seasons, leaving SoDak in winter, passing the "'Villes" of Loui and Nash through late fall, then early fall through Chattanooga, flipping to almost a spring feel around Atlanta, and then reimagining summer in Florida.

I received an email from Hugh via the Big Island Ginger farm. Along with the note below, he wrote me to tell of a boy that he and his wife had adopted that had gone to meet his biological father and half-brother in the Philippines. Hugh's adopted son had eventually paid to put his half sibling through college.

Hi Dylan,

I suppose you are on your way to meet your bio dad. I wish you a good trip and a good experience. I think it's really cool that you will go see him. I suppose you know Ruhi is a special sort of guy. Please keep me updated. What you get from meeting Ruhi is pretty much up to you. You are always welcome here. hope to meet you someday. good luck and aloha, Hugh

Along the way, I had great conversations with friends and family; Con, Jer, Lena, Julio, my pops, mom, old rowing and childhood buddies, my brothers-in-law, and Irene. All friends and family had positive encouragement to share, and we talked about feelings and expectations while keeping a calm sense of humor about the entire situation and journey.

In some ways, it seemed like a big deal. In others, it wasn't too major, as the search had been completed; this was simply the post-race finisher's beer. Irene asked if I could find out any health history and any other information about the other potential bio half sibling, Adam.

I had a clear mind as I pulled in late to Myakka State Park next to the gator pond. It was dark, jungly, and mosquito-ridden. I crashed out in my pickup, with plans to meet Ruhi in the morning at his daily breakfast spot. It was a sunny and fresh morning as I checked out with the gate staff, picked up a coloring book for Zu, and rolled southwest toward Venice.

I took a right turn over a waterway bridge onto the peninsula that was Venice, with ocean to the right and waterway to the left. As I pulled into the parking spot outside the little bakery, two thousand-plus miles recently under my belt, I could see through the open door the owner behind the counter and a small-statured man in a blue sweater with frizzy white hair somewhere between Albert Einstein's and Doc Brown's from *Back to the Future*.

BREAKFAST AND BIKES

I can't recall our exact first words as I approached them with my mask covering my face (standard COVID safety procedure), but I can picture Ruhi's blue eyes, face weathered by the elements, and tenderhearted smile, as he said, perhaps, "Hello, Dylan?"

He introduced me to his friend and bakery owner, Jim, a jovial man from the Chicago area with the thick, "da Beeaarzz" accent. Ruhi and Jim asked if I was hungry. Yes, thanks. Jim then told me what Ruhi had each morning: an egg scramble with some breakfast potatoes and toast. I ordered the "Ruhi special" with some added goat cheese spread on top.

We sat outside at a two-top as some groups of older cyclists stopped in and the next-door karate studio opened up for the day. Ruhi knew everyone who passed, and shared kind greetings. He had a familiar style that looked comfortable and functional; clean shorts, wool socks under his green rubber Birkies (randomly, I had the exact same pair), and he packed a small bag clipped to his waist with his vital belongings, including a neon biker's cap he would throw on when we headed out a bit later.

Over breakfast we talked a bit about the trip down and Venice but mostly enjoyed, in my opinion, the very tasty meal. Ruhi had described Jim as a quality chef and a very giving man. To Ruhi, the taste of the food was unimportant, as he made clear it was a matter of fuel and nourishment for his body.

I asked Ruhi if it was all right if Jim was willing to take our picture. They both obliged, and we took a picture of our first meeting standing next to the table outside. In the photo, I stand towering above Ruhi's smaller and aged frame. Our shoulders and lower legs look like mirror images, his with a few more years on them and mine a stretched-out version seemingly twice the size.

Ruhi was efficient with his eating, and I was still finishing up as he was exchanging salutations to Jim and looking to start the day. This dichotomy in pace—seeming slow but moving efficiently—would become my norm as I tagged along with Ruhi for the next twenty-four hours. I settled up with Jim and thanked him for the delicious food. Ruhi navigated me to a parking spot on the road next to the cafe, and I helped to tighten his bike rack back on using one of my bike-specific tools. From there, we literally rolled out, Ruhi on his pink cruiser with plastic storage crate on back, and me on the orange gravel bike I had hauled down in the back of my pickup.

KINDNE∬ ROUND∫

We biked across the street to the tobacco shop, where Ruhi picked up some papers for a friend and spoke warmly to the owner, a former military higher-up. Upon leaving, Ruhi touched his hand and told him to take good care, which seemed a bit of an odd gesture to a burly, cigar shop-owning military man. Once outside the door, he conveyed to me that the owner had just lost his wife, and was a good man who was struggling. We cruised on.

Ruhi would give me simple directions: "We'll turn right here," or "traffic sometimes comes fast from that lane."

I just went with it. I was thinking it had been a while since I had just rolled with no agenda, no real plan, or really any idea of where we were heading—and it was okay. I was slowing down to his pace, physically and mentally. It was comfortable and felt easy.

Ruhi told me he had been hit on his bike recently, but that most drivers were bike-conscious. Good to know, I thought—he had no idea that I was a fairly strong bike rider, he didn't ask and I didn't brag on myself. In fact, later on he would coach me on where on the road I should safely ride as he nearly crashed due to excess sand in the bike lane.

We turned into a small apartment complex and he told me he was going to look for a friend. An older gentleman was trimming some palm branches and tidying up, and Ruhi approached him, with me flanking behind. He introduced me to the landlord as he had with Jim, "This is my supposed biological son, Dylan."

I talked with the owner of the apartments, Gary, a very kind gentleman who spoke fondly of Marc. Ruhi walked away, looking for his friend. Gary filled me in on his family spread out over the world, who would not be connecting over Thanksgiving but hoped to be together in the near future. He smiled and said how kind a man Marc was. Around then, an older lady on a large trike, her small Pomeranian in the basket behind her seat, rolled in the driveway.

"Hi, Marc," she exclaimed. He introduced me again. She and the apartment owner were both amazed at hearing his biological son was standing in front of them. They agreed how neat it was that we had found each other, and that I had come to visit.

Ruhi's introduction had a gentle and kind but flat affect, more matter-of-fact than overjoyed pride, but that was to be expected. I felt comfortable and was just absorbing what I could. He passed the papers he'd picked up at the cigar shop over to his friend, and we were back on the bikes rolling out. Once down the road, he told me she struggled to afford them so he was happy to help.

IN HIꟙ ELEMENT

Our next stop was Ruhi's small apartment, which was an old Spanish-looking stucco building with eight or so apartment units scattered in multiple stories. Once inside, we removed our shoes and he showed me his living room, with the futon he usually slept on, a small kitchen, one bedroom, and bathroom. It was clean, tidy, and simple. He seemed to have just what he needed, and not much more.

Ruhi played Bob Dylan on his small, wall-mounted TV using YouTube. *Blood on the Tracks* came on, an album a college friend had gifted me in my early twenties. Ruhi mentioned something about how Bob Dylan hadn't always been honest—that he had changed his name after being influenced by the poet Dylan Thomas, but had denied this truth later in life.

He shared that a friend helped him to purchase a tablet so he could more easily write, because it was larger than his phone, but it had an autocorrect setting that was not helpful, and he had not succeeded in downloading a dictionary he had hoped to be able to use. I asked if I could take a look, and while he made some pourover coffees rectified the problems. I showed him where the dictionary was and, under settings, that the autocorrect was now turned off. He thanked me, and we took the coffees to the back patio.

As we started to visit, I took out the journal gifted from my sixth-grade student. I asked if he minded at all if I jotted some notes. I didn't feel impatient in needing to get information and questions answered, I just wanted to be sure I made some notes on what he chose to share. I mentioned Irene being curious about health history and about Adam. He said he had been diagnosed with CLL, Chronic Lymphatic Leukemia, and skin cancer, and that his eyes were degenerating. He described his parents' passing from major strokes, saying his father "went to sleep at ninety-six and his mother was put to sleep at seventy-seven years old."

Ruhi told me his father had sold newspapers as a kid in Atlantic City in the 1930s. He was the eighth or ninth child of twelve. He shared what he knew about Adam, saying he'd been adopted by another family upon his birth sometime in the early 1980s in Anacortes, Washington. Adam's mother, he said, "didn't want to be a mother and had another son, Kyle." Adam had lived in the mountains of Washington state before he committed suicide in his early twenties. Years later, his mother, Deborah, gave Ruhi a brown paper bag with articles about Adam's death. Adam was a sensitive boy who had been bullied, and his adoptive parents felt guilty about his death, Ruhi said.

He then went on to talk more about family history, saying that his mother's mother came to this country all by herself, not knowing her exact age. A relative had gotten her to the harbor, where she had boarded a boat. He said the entire family had ties to the czar of Russia, and been killed in the Bolshevik Revolution. Ellis Island had an address for a family member, "Bush," and she had attempted to reach out to them.

About this time, as seemed to be a common theme throughout our time together, a neighbor lady came out to the patio and Ruhi stopped his train of thought and introduced us. This time during introduction, I was his "possible biological son." The neighbor was nurse and a talker who liked to share stories about her work, and it seemed they often shared time together on the patio. She had no idea Marc had any kids, but was happy we were together. We elicited this reaction multiple times over the day we would spend together.

I finished my cup while talking with the neighbor, as Ruhi didn't say much and headed toward the back door. He told me later that she could talk for a while, and it was best to keep moving. He asked if I would like to walk to the beach. Yes, that would be great.

SUBJECTIVE INDIFFERENCE

On the way, as we cut through some back allies and walked by expensive properties, Ruhi told me about caring for his father during the last phase of his life. His dad, Floyd, asked him, "Marc, am I the reason that you are the way you are?"

"No, Dad, it's not because of you," Ruhi had reassured his ailing father.

We had been occasionally talking while on the move, with large amounts of unspoken quiet time, especially by my standards. Then, in one moment of directness that stands out as much as any during our time together, he turned to me and said that he was not going to make his father feel bad. From his perspective, it wasn't necessary. He said that after he told Floyd it wasn't his fault, his father's eyes welled up and they embraced.

During one of our earlier phone conversations, Ruhi had told me about a memory of a time after his mother passed, when he was seated at the kitchen table with his father. Floyd had asked him, "Marc, can we just accept each other as humans?" Ruhi replied, "Yes, Dad."

These stories seemed to carry weight for Ruhi, though he wouldn't equate or express this. Quantitative data and qualitative descriptive data of feelings didn't seem to take up brain space in his mind, even though these two things have high importance in the active and storage space of my neurology.

Regardless, I knew his sentiment would be that it didn't matter. I wanted to ask what felt like obvious questions, such as how did you feel, or did you imagine someday you would be sharing this story with someone like me? But I was fast learning that not only would these questions fail to spark continued conversation, they would just frustrate Ruhi. He would say to me, in an almost pleading voice, "Dylan, I don't want to be rude, but it doesn't matter."

When it comes to what matters, the gravity or quantitative measurement of importance seems to be highly subjective. What mattered to me might not have mattered to him, and vice versa. Either I could feel a bit of resentment and a competitive need to prove to him that it did matter, or I could make a conscious choice to attempt to accept his indifference and move on, step by step, toward the calm Gulf Coast. I went with the latter.

CHAPTER THIRTY-ONE

AN ENDLESS OCEAN VIEW

We slipped our sandals off at the sand. It was a familiar tradition my mom had educated all us kids about from an early age—you go barefoot on the beach, toes in the sand, and find some healthy time for "grounding." He asked me if I wanted to jump in the water, as I'd indicated I would at the breakfast table.

Ruhi sat near a tuft of grass growing up on a sandy bump. He talked about how much the coastline had changed and been developed, pointing out the high-rise hotels flanking us to the left and right. The tone and disgust in his voice sounded exactly like my pops, Johnny. He often expressed a similar longing for the California coast and other natural places that had fallen victim to development. I had heard this spiel about man's endless desire to build and take throughout my life, and found truth in it, but also thought, well what would Ruhi or Johnny have done if given the opportunity? Plus, I thought sarcastically, it didn't matter—until it does matter.

I set my gear next to him and headed down to the salty water, warm to me, cold to locals, and swam out into the easy rollers. After ten minutes or so, I popped out and back towards him. He said, "that's all the longer you wanted to swim?" I told him I'd go a bit longer, but it was hard not to analyze what he seemed to have input on, and what he didn't seem invested in or phased by.

Not once had he asked a question about who I was or my family story, but he questioned the length of time I spent in the Gulf waters. Ruhi was content hanging and watching walkers cruise by. I jumped back in and paddled a while longer, connecting the salt water to past memories in the Pacific off the coasts of Oregon, Hawaii, and Cali. The cycle of water and of life, both have strange ways of circling back at certain moments.

FAMILIAR NATURAL PACE/ LOVE TRIANGLE

After walking back to his place, Ruhi asked if I wanted to bike around the peninsula and go check out the boardwalk. He pointed it out, a mile or so down the beach. Of course, this was right up my alley. It was easy for me to match and enjoy the pace at which he moved through the day. All my life I had been jokingly criticized for moving from one task to the next, trying to fit in as much as possible. At other times, it wasn't jokes but legitimate frustration when others felt they were being pushed or subject to unfair expectations. When I was rolling with Ruhi, it was natural.

We cruised off on our bikes toward the boardwalk. I had been patiently quiet, more looking to absorb than forcing conversation. But on the bike, I started asking him questions about his life. I started with the most token, cliché question: Had he been in love? Ruhi shared a story about a woman he had deep feelings for, and she had reciprocated. She was caught in a triangle, though, as she had been together with a rich man, who she eventually married, and he could provide an extravagant life for her. Ruhi stayed in contact with her throughout the years, and at pivotal moments when she had considered a life with him, he had supported her and steered her back to her wealthy husband.

It was strange to hear the man who gave me my DNA talk about feelings he had throughout his life for a woman other than my mom, but I was able to disconnect and simply listen. I could be a pseudo-stranger as

I listened to this somewhat typical story of shared love versus pursuit of a comfortable life. This was *Pride and Prejudice* via beach air on bikes; I'm not sure if Ruhi was Wickham, but he lacked the greens of Darcy for certain.

DISAGREEMENT WITH
THE DEEP STUFF

We locked our bikes near the boardwalk and cruised over to a covered area en route to the boardwalk. Ruhi stopped to light up one of his tobacco rolled cigarettes, as he did whenever we stopped for a moment. He talked to me about the spiritual realm.

His was an almost *Matrix*-like approach to life, with a belief that the physical bodies we inhabited were temporary and insignificant. He said he thought he was potentially reaching his last phase of life, as if approaching his final chapter of reincarnation. He mentioned past friends who had suffered throughout their lives, and how they had accepted the burden of their circumstances based on a belief of previous mistakes they had lived in previous lives.

He was knowledgeable and interesting. I found, as I had previously, that when I would make my attempt to understand or agree with him, his typical response would start with, "no." It's like this or that, he would say, in disagreement and following up with backhanded education. I felt a sense of frustration in moments, but could sizzle it with the perspective that it wasn't worth an argument in the moment. It was simply more purposeful to listen.

Based on his writings and his life in general, the pivotal question for me was, "Was it worth it?" Did this life of traveling, wandering, pushing to experience as many things in life as possible to be better equipped to write about it, provide him with joy and purpose? When I posed this type of question, his simple reply was, "Dylan, it doesn't matter."

It seemed like a cop-out. Anyone could go through life doing as they pleased, with no repercussions, and rationalize that they were pursuing a truth and connection to God—but was it the most selfish of acts? His response to the question of selfishness seemed to be that, yes, it was selfish. But he believed he was, in a sense, without choice, as God had predetermined his pathway.

"So therefore," I asked, "there was no individual choice?"

Again, "No, Dylan, it's not like that. That's not important."

I found keeping a kind sense of humor to be pivotal in our interactions. We were communicating—and the process was more important than the product.

We walked out on the boardwalk and watched a fisherman land a large Gulf fish after ten minutes of fighting it, pulling it up to the elevated dock. Ruhi cautioned me to back up and mind the fishermen and women as we posed for a picture. Off the end, we spotted a dolphin below playing in the easy rollers, naturally in its element.

ROLLING ON

We cruised on down the one-lane road, the changing weather patterns washing the sand on and off. He coached me on how to ride my bike. At first, I fought back—if there was one area where I might have superseded ability, it was bike handling. But I humored him, simply tucking in behind him as ongoing cars passed.

He politely asked if I would like to stop and take another swim away from the busier part of the beach, where a woman was collecting clams in the shallow waters. Continuing on bikes, we rolled through some native beach grassland onto a bike path mirroring the canal. He told me the canal had been built during the Civilian Conservation Corps camps to allow for naval access and protection.

I was familiar with CCC, as my grandfather served in the Black Hills of SoDak to support his family, and the Oregon Youth Conservation Corps, where I'd been a member and later crew leader, was based on the same concept. After a long straight stretch we took our only stop circling the peninsula to rest. It was also the only time I heard Ruhi cuss. "Dylan, I need to stop," he said, "my ass is getting sore."

For dinner, he gave two options, some takeout Asian food or Subway sandwiches. I asked him to choose, and he went with the Asian takeout, adding it was a nice, family-run business. He motioned to the nearby field and explained the Barnum circus had used it as their winter home, animals and all. Remnants of some structures, various bar apparatuses, were still on site.

Ruhi asked if I would like to catch the sunset from the beach. I said, oh ya, that would be great. He thought if we snagged the food and headed back to his place to eat quickly, we would make the sunset. When we were in Honolulu, Keena and I had made it our nightly ritual to head to Ala Wai Park to catch the sunset for a chance at witnessing the "green flash." I'd enjoyed watching the sun set over the "sea of plains" as often as possible for the past ten years, but it had been a minute since I looked to the west to watch it set over the ocean.

Over our month of correspondence, it had become evident that Ruhi and I both enjoyed capturing sunsets on our adventures, as we had shared many photos of them through email and text. On the way to the food, we passed by a homeless man who Ruhi casually said hello to, as he did with seemingly every person we saw, and rolled on without hesitation.

Not far up the trail, two large tortoises crossed our path and Ruhi suggested I take a picture to show my daughter, so I did. The homeless man, with all his supplies, cruised by, this time saying, "Hi, Marc." After he was out of hearing distance, Ruhi said he was a nice man who worked very hard at a local mechanic shop and who chose to live his homeless lifestyle, as he appreciated the freedom it presented.

I ordered the same meal as Ruhi, a shrimp-veggie dish, and he checked in with the owners behind masks and plexiglass. Ruhi asked about how their family was handling the pandemic, and how their kids were doing with school. We continued to fall easily in place spending time together, and pedaled back to his place to share a mostly silent meal before a walk back to the beach for sunset.

SON-ʃeT

Again removing our shoes, we walked toward a tall, strong-looking man with a camera on the beach. Ruhi introduced me as his "biological son" and the man gave me a kind smile and said, "pleased to meet you." I headed toward the grassy knoll Ruhi had perched on earlier and set my gear down for an evening dip in the ocean, making it a trifecta.

Once we were out and drying in the fading light, Ruhi sat next to me told me the man with the camera had been a prison guard on death row in New York. Captured by prisoners, he had been beaten to death—and came back to life in the emergency room. He now lived alone and underwent electric stimulation treatments. Ruhi would help with them, to treat the pain. He photographed every sunset with the changing clouds and weather conditions.

The man had said we should have a clear and nice sunset. Watching the sunset over the ocean is akin to staring at the crackling campfire. They're both forms of natural entertainment with a built-in social experience, and our shared appreciation for them runs deep within our bones, making it easy to enjoy with others without any expectations or obligations.

It seems equally acceptable to let the conversation flow or to sit in silence with another. There is no agenda, other than to pay witness, appreciate, and take in the natural environment. Pelicans, solo and in groups up to five, glided low, hovering over the water with a perfect sunset behind, creating a picturesque silhouette that I attempted to capture. As the sun fell into the water below, we saw no green flash but beautiful, 360-degree pink elephants on parade all around.

    I looked up to see Ruhi's friend had ventured down the beach to snap our picture. We thanked him, and he said he would email Marc the photos. Ruhi said in all the years they had known each other he had never seen him take a picture of other people, only the sunset. He was doing us a great kindness and service.

We walked back home, with some stars starting to appear above. It felt like a day spent in Africa or hiking in the mountains, where minutes seemed longer and more fulfilled because of an ability to be in the moment. At Ruhi's place, I made plans to go grab my pickup and head back to the park. He asked if I would like to stay, and warmly extended his extra, unused bedroom. I obliged, thanked him, and biked through the touristy downtown, lit up for the holiday season, to grab my pickup and head back. As I brought in my gear, including my guitar, he was stationed at his counter writing on his tablet.

CHAPTER THIRTY-TWO

INDIFFERENT PAIN

After I got set up, I casually asked Ruhi, "Do you mind if I strum some soft guitar?"

He had been transfixed on his tablet, I assume writing some of the poetry or stories I had received by email over the previous few weeks, upwards of five a night. He had not greeted me, or even looked up, for the ten-plus minutes I had been back at his place.

"No, Dylan, I would not care for that. I have listened to the greatest guitarist ever to play and anything else does not compare to this. I don't wish to be rude, but I do not want to hear anyone else."

His answer was honest and, according to typical social norms, rude. Here were two river forks merging into some turbulent rapids. My baseline of normalcy was the Moro circle game, a highlight of our family get-to-gethers and possibly our greatest family tradition, where we all were not only welcome to participate in music, but encouraged. Our circle game was an inclusive act of sharing and participating together—in essence, it was an audible form of love that took on the physical form of creation and artistry. Even if the music we created was not the best quality, it was enjoyed just the same. There was no judgment, no competitive nature, instead only acceptance, joy, and connection as we shared our art.

Hypothetically, having been raised by Ruhi would have been different. In his own words, he has given clarity to the idea that he was not meant for this world and would not have been able to provide the nurture a child would need and deserve. It seems, simply based on his relationship with his own father, Ruhi may never have been able to provide me with the outwardly expressed love and sense of togetherness I grew up with. I felt such an appreciation for the family dynamic I had been lucky to grow into with Johnny, Deb, my siblings, and our extended family, coupled with the families I had married into.

Within Ruhi's nature seemed to be an appreciation for music, based on his listening to Bob Dylan earlier, but also a sense of entitlement. For me, when I was really in tune with something—acoustic indie bands of the late nineties and early 2000s, NBA basketball, bike trails and touring—I always made an effort to include others who shared an interest but might not share my expertise, and I never shut them down when they tried to share their thoughts or ideas.

Right or wrong, he had a blatant disregard for any potential expertise of experience I might be willing and able to share. I couldn't understand why this man, who had made it a life mission to experience anything and everything to give him perspective to write his poetry and stories, was unwilling to allow me to share a piece of my art and myself with him. Me, his biological son. Me, who had listened, read, and been a part of all of his stories and writings, in a sense, hanging onto each word. Where was the reciprocation?

It was obvious that we had much different levels of tolerance for the art of others, and for the vulnerable places others might be willing to put themselves in to share the art. I was not a great musician—basic on the guitar, and poor at matching pitch. In fact, my lack of this ability was within my DNA. According to 23andMe, mom and all of my siblings were genetically predisposed to be able to match pitch, but I did not inherit this gene. Either it was a Moro dominant trait or, in my case, I got Ruhi's flip of the coin and not Deb's.

On our bike earlier, Ruhi was softly chanting/singing in a different language. He had a subdued but kind-sounding singing voice. When he finished, I asked if he liked to sing. He said it didn't matter, and we rolled on. Deb had been so steadfast and consistent in supporting my pursuit of any form of art, and had bred great confidence in me, even if it was modestly unfounded. I was writing from a young age, creating original songs later in life—even the drawings and photos I produced were highly praised, when an unbiased observer, I'm sure, would say they were decent at best. I always had a certain sense of self-awareness, but I appreciated her support.

It was clear that Ruhi did not feel compelled to provide any of the confidence nurture or stoking of my ego that the previous thirty-seven years may have deprived us of, for lack of proximity and knowing connection. It didn't matter—I didn't need his support for self-confidence. I simply wanted to share a part of my Moro family's love language, the gift of music. Not only did he not care for it, he didn't care to even have a taste of the experience.

I had made the pact with myself to tamper expectations, so I didn't have ill feelings about his lack of interest. It did, however, show me how drastically different we were, in so many ways. I had been nurtured to share and support others' art, it seemed he had selfishly gone about his pursuit of his own art and works to share with others, whether reciprocated or not.

In fact, his writing had a few ongoing themes. One seemed to be a general feeling of being unfulfilled, since his poetry had not been received and recognized in the mainstream because it had never been popular enough to be circulated among the masses. He spoke of a time he had been encouraged to send his writings to major publishers, where he had been told, "people should read your writings, but there is no financial market for us to publish them."

He seemed to have the type of regret that many people experience when they do not reach the maximum of their perceived potential in a passion-driven line of work. It was familiar to me. My pops Johnny had shared similar feelings about his music, and even mom Deb about children's stories. To a certain extent, I had felt the same in coaching or sharing songs.

The other theme of his writing was that he didn't know anything. Essentially, he wrote, humans did not possess the ability to understand the truth and godly sentiment he had spent his life pushing to fulfill. It seemed to be a self-supported loop of understanding, one that provided an out to everything, to believe that humans are incapable of knowing or understanding anything divine. Tough to nail down truth and hypocrisy with these coinciding angles.

Another theme was that of silence. In much of his writing about encounters with monks, spiritual Indians, and random people met in desert travels through the Southwest or commune living, he told about sitting with them in silence and then, after a long amount of time, breaking into gut-wrenching laughter or welling up tears together, without any words shared. He told many stories of hearing great people speak, only to walk away early or alone into nature, where he would sit and consider what had been said. His implication was that he had a greater truth already inside, though he never put this in words.

This place of having a self-perceived greater scope on truth or opinion felt familiar to me. I believe most people deal with a sense of judgment and entitlement, but my natural state seems to supersede that of most. It's one of my most poignant character flaws. Was this genetic? Did Ruhi hook me up? Or was it just random? Either way, the dude didn't want to hear my minimal musical skills, and I could accept that. Plenty others throughout my life did find joy in sharing a tune, and that was more than enough. His loss.

CHAPTER THIRTY-THREE

SPILLING OVER

Ruhi was on the futon with some pie and ice cream, watching an old BBC *Sherlock Holmes*. He offered me some, and I helped myself. His fridge was modest, clean, and had the necessities to sustain. I had asked Ruhi earlier if he enjoyed cooking, and he said he was indifferent, it was just a means to provide fuel. That being said, he seemed to be enjoying the late-night sweet snack (it also reminded me of vintage Johnny Moro, as he too indulges in ice cream and pie every night). After finishing my bowl, he asked if I would care for more. I said, "No thanks, I'm good. It was perfect."

"What is perfect? I've never known this word."

"Oh, I just meant I'm full, happy, and satisfied. Just a misspoken word."

"Well, then use those words, don't use words unless they describe what you actually intend them to. The only perfect I know is God, and I have not even experienced that perfect."

I felt the competitive need to put up a bit of a fight. For me, this had been a long period of biting my tongue and letting things go. It seemed like an arbitrary point to argue—I understood his intent and agreed, words should be used accurately, but commonplace conversation should allow for some flexibility. Also, his seemingly inconsistent argumentative moments were throwing me for a bit of a loop.

It had been an awesome day, but there hadn't been much conversational agreement. Instead, there had been one-sided points of facts, and acknowledgments of what I or others didn't seem to understand. It wasn't so much that he was wrong, but I was thrown by his tone and an almost demand that I fit in his box of acceptable actions and words. Conversely, I felt unsettled about the box of a life he had chosen for himself in the first place. I took his advice, decided it doesn't matter, and we wished each other a restful night and crashed.

In the bedroom, I wrote a bit in my journal and read the intro to *Night*, the Holocaust account book Ruhi had given me earlier in the day, saying that he had once met author Elie Wiesel. I told him my sister and mother-in-law had gone to hear him speak in Sioux City, Iowa, and were amazed at his stories. Passing the book to me was a kind gesture by Ruhi, as he'd gotten it himself from one of the box book exchanges stationed on random trails throughout town. As I thanked him, he dismissed my gratitude a bit, and said, "Dylan, I have no possessions. This book is not mine, so please take it to read."

WHEN LEAST EXPECTED

I woke the next morning and Ruhi was up typing on his tablet. He had told me that he often spent much of the night up writing, and his quota of emailed poetry and stories provided evidence, coming throughout the night—midnight, 2 a.m., 4 a.m. I quietly got ready for the day, and he asked me how I slept.

"Almost perfect," I replied with a smile.

"Dylan, are you being funny?"

"Yes, I am," I replied, and we both shared a smile.

We talked about the daily plans. He had his surgery scheduled for early afternoon, and the neighbor lady had asked if I would take him to his appointment. I would be happy to, I had committed. I thought the least I could do was to be his ride to and from the appointment. The morning of the surgery, he caringly suggested that I might get an earlier start on the road home and to visit a close childhood friend from my days in Plankinton, South Dakota—Vessel, now living in South Carolina. He told me it was kind that I was willing to help him, but that he was fine and it would be better to drive while there was daylight and to have time with my friend in the evening.

I agreed and we set out to walk toward the cafe where we had first met the previous day, thus completing our twenty-four hours of time together. Walking by store windows, he was quiet, but pointed out a couple of Christmas ornaments in a gift shop, unprompted.

"Your wife might like that ornament."

It was hard to understand the inner workings of his mind, as the minute I started to accept that he operated on a different plane, without much care for the material world or incongruent to the socially acceptable way most humans moved throughout their day and lives, he would point out an ornament that my wife would appreciate. When least expected, he had feelings and thoughtful, selfless moments, it seemed.

The man emptying the trash bags on Main Street just down from the shop immediately and joyfully greeted Marc. Ruhi introduced us.

"This is my son, Dylan."

With a big smile, the man greeted me warmly, and after Ruhi asked about his family we moved on. I mentioned that I noticed how he introduced me, and how it was different than he had been doing it over the past twenty-four hours.

"It is easier if I introduce you this way, he is a simple man," he said. "This will not confuse him. It is important to know how best to communicate with others."

When you least expect it, I thought, with an internal chuckle. This wasn't an acceptance of our relationship so much as it was an act of kindness meant to get on the level of the kind garbage man—and that was okay. We strolled back after another nice meal to start the morning, and stopped by the post office to mail Sandra, Ruhi's sister, our family Christmas card as promised after Ruhi helped with her address. I had given him our family holiday card the day before, along with a few pictures. He had accepted them with a bit of awkwardness again, saying, "Dylan, I don't want to be rude, but I have no use for such things."

I told him that was fine, he could toss them or whatever he'd like, I just wanted to share them. That morning I had noticed the card as the sole object on the front of his fridge. When least expected.

I gathered my belongings and packed up, he asked if he could make me a small bag of snacks for the road. He tucked in the fortune cookies from the Chinese takeout, a couple Ricola drops (I had asked for one the day before as well), some cookies and fruit. After loading up, he walked out front with me. This was the moment that epitomized the entire trip. I am not an overly outwardly emotional person, but I could feel some emotions welling up. Happy, sad, not really sure, a bit of both. It just felt like a magnetism between two entities as we gave each other a farewell hug, his small frame wrapped with my larger. I sensed that he felt a reciprocal feeling. He presented me with a small golden angel lapel pin and said, "For Zuzu."

The man with no possessions was giving my daughter, his genetic granddaughter, a gift of remembrance. We thanked each other for the time together, and he smiled at me with his eyes closed in the midmorning sun as I pulled away. It felt good.

On the way out of town, I stopped at the store and bought matching ornaments for Keena, Debra, and my mother-in-law Karen. I told the shop owner what had brought me to Venice, she started to tear up. She said how hard it had been not to see her family back in England over the holidays, but that my story had warmed her heart. I snagged a stuffed dolphin for Zu, like the one we had seen from the boardwalk, and headed back over the bridge away from the peninsula. I felt content, and played the Avett Brothers as the sunroof peeled open.

The time had gone, in many ways, as I had hoped and foreseen. It wasn't perfect, but it was memorable, necessary, and fulfilling. I had found Ruhi, and we had shared time in person. Life was good and, as when I was a child in school, I was thankful for it.

CHAPTER THIRTY-FOUR

ROLLING HOME INTO PRESENT

Driving home, I spoke with many of the same family and friends I had on the way down, updating them on the experience. I talked with Irene, and we shared an easy conversation. Later on we video chatted, showing each other our homes and family. She and her family are easy to talk with, and I have a great appreciation for them.

She shared handwritten letters Ruhi had written to her mother in 1982, after she had made him aware of her pregnancy with Irene. His message seemed to change—in the first letter he advised her to think of not having the child, and in a subsequent letter the next day he had accepted that it was her decision, but said he would not be able to be a stable father figure for the child. I asked Irene how she felt.

"Indifferent," she replied.

I tried to convey how it felt to be with him in person, and to accurately understand who he was and is—a paradox of sorts. I told her if she ever wanted to meet him in person, I would be happy to go with her. She thanked me, saying maybe someday, but that she was content for now with her family and talking with me and my family.

THE GENETIC I DON'T KNOW

I don't feel now as if I have answers to the nature-versus-nurture debate. I am me because of my family, my genetics, my choices, my motivations, my desires, and my presence and future. I can now tell Zu what I know of my story, and about what contributes to what she is made up of, as well.

For thirty-five years, I knew my exact genetic makeup, but all that was changed with a DNA test. For two years I pursued a quest to find a wandering poet with the pen name Ruhi. A three-word Google search, "Ruhi Poet Cornell," led me to an article about ginger and, inevitably, my biological father. There does not seem to be an end all, be all answer to why things shake out the way they do.

I now have at least one other half sibling, with a family she cares about, who shares a quarter of the same DNA. That's just as much as I share with the three siblings I was raised with, roughly twenty-five percent. We are not a perfectly nuclear family, but we accept that there may be no such thing, and it doesn't matter.

Ruhi continues to send daily poems and stories, and includes my mom on the contact list that he writes to.

Today my mom shared with me the email she had written to Ruhi:

Hello Marc,

I simply want to say how grateful I am that you include me in your emails. I enjoy your writing immensely while I sit by the fire every morning. Unique is how I remember you, and how you made me feel. I told Dylan once you worshipped me, poor choice of words. You made me feel like a dancer, a beautiful presence full of grace. It's okay that you don't remember me. I am glad to know you now inside, and for Dylan to be with you was so helpful. I do have chests of drawers of what I call treasures. Pictures, cards, and letters. The book of poetry you gave me, typed, was titled, *Petals of Light* by Ruhi. I search for it and pray it is here, not yet. (heart) I think of you with renewed interest and hope you find good health and a peaceful home.

Your friend, Debra

She attached a picture of herself with a candle and small Christmas tree. Ruhi's reply:

> Thank you, Debra, for the photo of you & I am glad you like reading what I write.

> May John & you have a good New Year.
> Love Ruhi.

I've joked with Keena that, based on the randomness of finding Ruhi, I would say there is at least a ten percent chance that Ruhi someday lives with my mom and dad as a roommate.

For Christmas this year, my mom drew my name in the family gift exchange and gifted me with a handmade poem and song book titled *It Seems to Me* by John David Moro. Below the title is a picture of Johnny restringing his guitar. Inside the cover is the list of songs and poetry: "I Can See My Life," "Plantvedanta," "Blow those Clouds Away," "Politician," "Absurd Words," "Hurry Hurry Hurry," "When I Was Younger," "Jimmy Come Back to Me," "Heaven," "Blame It On Me," "Pretend," "Look Out to Sea," "Guess I'll See Ya," "Fantasy," "Eternal Story of Life." Just reading the titles triggers many of the tunes of the songs in my mind. I've spent thirty-eight years of my life listening to them. Debra had hand-typed each song and poem from my dad's treasure trove of writings, which she had uncovered while searching for *Petals of light* by Ruhi.

Petals of Light remains missing, Ruhi has been found, and I will have my pops Johnny's songs humming in my mind until my last breath. I'll keep his book of poems and songs next to my journal filled with notes on my genetic search.

As I read my dad's poems and songs, I see similarities to Ruhi's writings. I may be half Jewish and not half Spanish/Italian, but my nurturing seems to have equipped me with the ability to accept my new truth of who

I am and what makes me up just fine. Perhaps to Ruhi it doesn't matter, but to me it does, and I am now content.

My dad signed his book, "Hope you enjoy these and know there are more to come, Dad."

As I type his words below, I hum the ballad in my head while Zu peacefully naps on the couch, her genetics promoting cell growth and replication nurtured by her South Dakota born-and-bred mom and half Jewish South DakOregonian pops.

Look Out to Sea
© 1983 John Moro
Look, look out to sea...the waves have been playing a song for a
million years
Do you know the tune?
Of the wind, blowing through the tops of the trees
Are you in the right key?
Ah...These things are so beautiful
There's no need to say
Ah...These things are so beautiful
Each in their own way
Take from me...all the songs I yield and sing to you every night
A sweet melody.....About my life...it seems to be huddled
in strife
But still simple and free
Of the pains that are paying the debt of my reality
Will they ever be pleased?
We're signing a song and it's beautiful
Doing it in our own way
We're living life and it's beautiful
Each in our own way.

And we try and we try to get along but it seems like things just
go wrong

Maybe someday will if this cup right over my head and I'll be
better off dead

Guess I'll see Ya

Been thinking about all of the good times we used to have

When we were together there was no time for feeling sad

When you went away, you said you wanted to be free

But now each night, I wonder whether that can be

We've seen the stars at night and the falln' rain

There's been a lot of times when things have been right

Now it's time for a change

Guess I'll see ya…

I look inside my mind why do I do what i do

It is me or just a reflection of you?

And the past…seems to take up a lot of my time

Then I realize that it's all inside my mind…

We've seen the stars at night and the fallin' rain

There's been a lot of times when things have been right

Now it's time for a change

I guess I'll see ya

EPILOGUE

Recently Johnny S. sent me over fifty pages of Ruhi's poems and traveling stories from earlier in his life; titled *Book of My life Experiences* by Marc Frank. Ruhi told me he had worked on this writing in a Lake Oswego coffee shop every day for a period of time. I also ordered four copies of *Clouds of Light* by Marc Ruhi Frank from the Sequel Book store in Enumclaw, Washington via of all places Amazon's online used bookstore. These books harbor the smell of having been on shelf since their publishing in 1978 in affiliation with Portland State University and East-West University of Brahmavidya Gurukula. His poetry—was—available on the internet, but having purchased the only remaining copies for Irene, Deb, Ruhi, and Zu it once again vanished without a trace.

Finding Clouds of Light prompted me search for Marta's French writing about Mother Teresa, of which Amazon had one copy. When my mom opened Ruhi's poetry book I sent her she said, "Thanks, I don't recall any of these from Ruhi. I like this one."

YOU ARE ME

Your temple is my head.
I close my eyes to see it.
Your holiness is my feet
to walk the earth.
And Your divine love
is my heart's throbbing.

I shared my writings with Ruhi and my mom as I worked through the editing process. I had told Ruhi I was working on writing my story of DNA testing and the subsequent journey to track him down. He said he would like to read my story, and would provide feedback if something legitimately stuck out to him. He made it clear that he would not provide false feedback, and only comment if he felt so inclined.

Here's Deb's feedback upon reading some of the manuscript:

I like hearing you tell, and realize I never knew the depth of your
determination when I left you hopelessly thinking he was gone.
And you convinced me if I heard his voice, I would most likely
recognize his speaking voice and mannerism with words!

    Love you more and Moro. What an interesting and
mixed-up combination of mind and body and spirit/heart. You
score highest of all in your passion for life.

Love,
Mom

Well done seems accurate and honest with yourself,
righteous stubborn competitor
pushing another into a potentially uncomfortable situation for
selfish reasons and forcing others to reconcile choices (heart)
Relentless is the word is use to describe you

And I always love you
Sometimes I think we taught you better when you push too hard, wink.

My response:

Haha, maybe it's nature

And here's what Ruhi had to say:

Dear Dylan,

I read what you wrote. You are putting together your life story.
The moment you inwardly feel integrated, then you can feel at
peace. Do write it out—it's a long process of knowing self.

Love,
Ruhi

After I shared with Ruhi the poems I had written online when searching for him:

MARC FRANK <marcruhifrank8@gmail.com>
Sun 10/11/2020 3:11 PM

Difficult for me to feel how strong was your longing to
find Ruhi.

Please under no circumstances neglect your family. They
come first in your life. Yes!

Finally Marta's words:

Dear Dylan,
Your note is a very pleasant surprise to me.

I see in your writing the talent passed to you from Marc.

So glad to know that you are going to continue writing
and yes

I give you my blessings wishing you to have a clear vision
and pure inspiration...

Writing for me has to do a lot with intuition. A space open
to that which is beyond words.

I also want to say that it made me very happy to see you
both together something so beautiful was happening to him and
you .

Subject: Re: Early in the morning

Hi dear Marc,
Thank you for sharing Dylan's letter.

His search eventually led him to you and hopefully brought
him peace.

It is that we want to know the root from which we originated.

I like his writing and the story is pretty absorbing. Be well my friend.

Love,
M.

ACKNOWLEDGEMENTS

To Zu for giving me ultimate purpose, inspiration to be better, fun and learning in every moment, and for being the only other human to share my specific genetic code. Looking at your resting eyelashes and perfect cheeks while you catch some zzz's I start to truly understand love and balance in life. Three-taps to Keen for supreme support and honest love, tough when I need it and always genuine. Your work ethic, selflessness, and the mom and wife that you are each day are my guiding light.

Mom—your unconditional love and caring heart have given me the ultimate life. Thank you for being with me on this journey with honest emotions and support. Dad—you have been my best friend through life. I owe everything I am to you choosing to love and raise me and our family--and I can still kick your butt in basketball.

Hey Jer you've been with me all of my days and understand better than anyone the full scope of our lives together. I love you and am so proud of the mother you have become, I hope this writing is positive and peaceful, thank you for allowing me to always be truthful, relentless, and crazy annoying--and still loving me. G, since day one, you've been a buddy I can check in with about whatever's free flowing in my brain, you bring balance and are so giving to the fam. Julio, the dude, I am proud to have you as a brother. I appreciate your gentle kind spirit, and am glad that you can dunk for the both of us, ha. Deebs, I am so grateful for your acceptance of all others, commitment to helping this world, willingness to share your talents, and genuine kindness. J-man, your positive energy is contagious, and I'm stoked to have you and that deep suave singing voice in the permanent circle game.

To my chosen fam, thanks for listening to my unrelenting BS and being willing to keep dealing with me. Karen, thanks for your willingness to have an honest relationship with me, providing a roadmap to selfless service, and for raising such an amazing family with Harvey. H-Todd, I appreciate your example of how a gentle father takes care of his loved ones and walking Keens down the aisle, dinkin flicka. Brook, you are the person all of us can go to with anything and be in a better place after talking with you. Jo-essay you keep me grounded and also get all of "it", looking forward to being dads together. Emo-Chris you can absorb my terrible jokes better than anyone. You have your pops authentic and kind spirit (your step back is also respectable). Clrrr-boom points, I truly appreciate your willingness to challenge me and bring another perspective. You are strong, wise, and responsible, thanks for dealing with all of my crap. Tunation-you helped to inspire Keen and I into some of the best decisions of our lives together, your wit and Tuna-tude help make life good, daily. Tone-I appreciate your positive spirit, intelligence, and willingness to jump into adventures and games. God-momma Holzy and Gma Lo for your love and humor. Gpa Jer and Gma D laughing and smiling down. Thank you all for helping me through this journey and being willing to share opinions. The Rage you will always inspire me to push towards my physical limits with a smile, you're in my heart.

JM, Ev, Jo-jo I am so proud of all of you for your unique energy and zest for living, thank you. Thanks for life and continued nurture to the Moro, Groeber, Brink, Olivas and Frank families. Gma and Gpa Moro, for teaching me fun and banter and how to fill a small space with love. Gram and Gramps Brink, you have modeled how best to grow old with the love of your life.

All of my cousins and Aunts and Uncles, each of you has given me something special through the years and I am so grateful to have you as family. Uncle Jimmy for being willing to honestly share at a pivotal moment, Aunt Tina and Aunt Diane for reminding me of my value in the Moro family. Aunt Norma, Nanc, Pat, Donna and Uncle Dean for allowing me to ask you questions and always supporting me unconditionally. Sally, Kar, Al, Autumn, Mind, Tif, Liz, and Knuty for being able to jump right back in at any point in life and instantly reconnect on a deep level of fun, love, and trust. John Carl, Mindy, Aaron, Sidney, and Emily seeing you populate as relatives online gave me belief and confidence. Ezra, Justin, Laramie, and all other extended cousins and significant others I'm happy to have you as family. Jeremy being my buddy cousin from day one on, what you continue to do for Grandma today is truly amazing. John and Chris, thanks for showing me what cool is and letting me jump in with you. Matt and Katie thank you for valuing family. Uncle you made our childhood great and I have your gene for never wanting to miss out on family fun. Aunt Kellea you have always been honest and genuine and showed me great strength and love. Brando, you remain my hero and I'm grateful for time we had together and you showing me how to have fun and live well.

Irene, Hoomi, precious Tulip, and Jolanta what an amazing future we can have together. Thank you for your willingness to correspond and support. Irene you may be the sole other human who fully understands this journey and I am so grateful you exist.

Con, cakes, and fam for being a lifelong buddy that can look big picture and enjoy adventure along the way. To Thunder, Wiz, T-High, Norm, Spar, Big-D, Nick(s), Ben(s), BTG, and all of my rowing buddies and coaches helping me to understand team and extended family. My friends through the years Justin, Jared, Jeff, Vess, Brad and Brandon, Travis, Wag, Nall, T, Benny, Hope, Jamie, Robert, Prairie, Joe, Toots, Jimmy, Anthony C, Al, BJ, Biggie, Richie, Laird, Sumo, Bindy, Molly, Bank St. buddy, Chadly, Mark, Lonnie, Blainer, Queen, Marcoe, and all those unnamed you know who you are. To my teacher friends that have been an active part of this search, much thanks for supporting me and being a soundboard throughout.

Will for being my big brother and Sherm for helping me and my big brother to have a continual voice of reason and loving guidance.

My parents buddies and bandmates who in turn are my buddies and have not only loved and supported my fam, but have been pivotal in its creation and successful continuation—Alan and Kels, Fred and Laur, Kelly and Suz, Vi, Mary E, JP and Gayle for putting the ability and confidence to write and share a story in my hands and mind, PG rolling a bike above, the Hales, Bobby and Gina for helping me build muscle and humor, and all others through the years and all of their beautiful children.

Trish and son thank you for helping my mom and I back in the early 80's, taking the time now, and letting us into your home to start the journey. Susan Anderson, later when corresponding you told me about your professor who advised you to include the little details in her writing. For my sake, thank goodness you did. Jenny Stockdale and Cornell University. Aloha, biker dude Hugh, Elvira, and Daniel much mahalo, your willingness to help and connect me to Ruhi made all the difference in our lives. Johnny Stallings your willingness to instantly give and receive authentic trust with a stranger promoted family connection. Jace and his story.

My cousins and family united through 23andMe and Ancestry. Beverly and JeTaunne for giving me hope and being willing to correspond and keep up. Janice W. Suzanne your support and willingness to correspond kept my motivation of possibility alive. Yifaht without your random suggestion my full story would not have been discovered, I am forever grateful. My Kadoka Jewish cousin, and fam, seeing you pop up made me believe again in the possibility. All those at 23andMe and Ancestry for providing a platform of connection and discovery.

Sandra, thank you for speaking with me and providing great framework and information about the Frank family.

Fiverr and Shelley Mann for your consistent kindness and patience, your talents provided clarity to this story. Isabel and the team at Bookbaby. Amazing eye, kindness, and photography of Lauren Roche. The inspiring

Saroo, author of *A Long Way Home*, your story gave me hope during my search.

You for taking the time to read. To all others not mentioned by name, you know the positive power of your support through this adventure and my life, I humbly thank you.

To Marta, your kindness and wisdom has shown a supreme positive light, thank you.

And to Ruhi, I set out in part to provide information to a man with whom I shared half of his genetics, in turn I found a uniquely kind and gentle-spirited friend. Again, I would not be here if not for you and your journey through life. Your written and spoken words have had great positive impact on many, and I am proud to know you. Thank you for your willingness to connect, may the rest of your journey be peaceful.

In the updated words of my Kindy self, "I am thankful that all of us are alive."

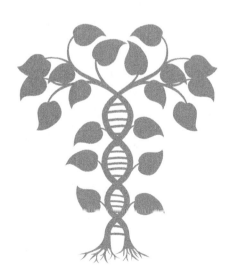

Made in the USA
Middletown, DE
25 August 2021